25-15

STUDIES IN CHRISTIAN WORSHIP 10

Music and Worship in the Anglican Church

The Living Liturgy at Pershore Abbey

Music and Worship in the Anglican Church 597—1967

By **PAUL CHAPPELL**
Vicar Choral of Hereford Cathedral

THE FAITH PRESS
7 TUFTON STREET, LONDON, S.W.1

FIRST PUBLISHED IN 1968

© *Paul Chappell, 1968*

PRINTED IN GREAT BRITAIN
in 11 point Garamond type
BY THE FAITH PRESS LTD.
LEIGHTON BUZZARD

SBN 7164 0055 3

DEDICATED TO

DR. GERALD KNIGHT AND CANON PETER MOORE

AND TO

THE DEAN AND CHAPTER OF HEREFORD CATHEDRAL

IN MEMORY OF

CANON PERCY DEARMER (1867–1936)

Introduction

This century has witnessed a renaissance, if not a revolution, in English Church music. The following chapters confirm this fact and also relate the use of secular musical styles in the service of the sacred. Particular attention has been given to the architectural setting of public worship. And the author believes that in the present pursuit of Church Unity, both the music and the liturgy of the Anglican Church has much to offer this modern age. He wishes to thank Canon Ronald Jasper and Father James Crichton, as well as the patience and the unfailing kindness of the Director of the Faith Press, for their initial encouragement in the writing of this book.

Contents

Abbreviations

AHB	– *Anglican Hymn Book*
AHC	– Ascherberg, Hopwood and Crew
AMR	– *Ancient and Modern Revised*
BH	– Boosey and Hawkes
BP	– Blandford Press
C	– Curwen
CFC	– *Carols for Choirs*
CH	– Chester
CMS	– Church Music Society (published by OUP)
EH	– *English Hymnal*
FP	– Faith Press
H	– Hinrichsen
HCS	– *Hymns for Church and School*
N	– Novello
OBC	– *Oxford Book of Carols*
OUP	– Oxford University Press
RSCM	– Royal School of Church Music
SB	– Stainer and Bell
SCH	– Schott
SPCK	– Society for Promoting Christian Knowledge

Acknowledgments

Church Information Office Publications, for extracts from *Music in Church: the Report of the Archbishops' Committee appointed in 1948* (Revised Edition, 1960).

Clarendon Press and the authors, for extracts from Ernest Walker's *A History of Music in England* (Revised Edition, 1952), and from Robert Bridges' *Collected Essays* XXI–XXVI (1935).

Dover Publications, for extracts from Charles Burney's *A General History of Music* (Modern Edition, 1957).

Epworth Press and the author, for an extract from Charles Cleall's *Music and Holiness*.

Faith Press and the author, for an extract from J. A. Lamb's *The Psalms in Christian Worship* (1962).

Messrs. A. & C. Black Limited and the author, for extracts from Owen Chadwick's *The Mind of the Oxford Movement* (1960).

Messrs. J. M. Dent & Sons Limited with Messrs. W. W. Norton and Company, for extracts from Thomas Morley's *A Plain and Easy Introduction to Practical Music* (edited by R. Alec Harman, 1963), and from Gustave Reese's *Music in the Renaissance* (1959).

Messrs. Faber & Faber Limited and the authors, for extracts from G. W. O. Addleshaw's and Frederick Etchells' *The Architectural Setting of Anglican Worship* (1948), from C. M. Ady's *The English Church* (1940), from Gabriel

Hebert's *Liturgy and Society* (1935), and from C. Henry Phillips' *The Singing Church* (1945).

The Order of St. Benedict, Collegville, Minnesota, for an extract from Joseph Gelineau's *Voices and Instruments in Christian Worship* (1964).

Messrs. Routledge & Kegan Paul Limited and the author, for an extract from Frank Ll. Harrison's *Music in Medieval Britain* (Second Edition, 1963).

Mr. Denis Stevens, for an extract from *Thomas Tomkins* (Macmillan, 1957).

Oxford University Press Limited, together with the authors and the editors, for extracts from *The New Oxford History of Music*, Volume III (edited by Dom Anselm Hughes and Gerald Abraham, 1961), from *Henry Purcell* (edited by Imogen Holst, 1959), and from the Preface (*The Music* by R. Vaughan Williams) to *The English Hymnal* (1906).

The quotations by S. S. Wesley on pages 89 and 90 are reproduced from *A Few Words on Cathedral Music* by S. S. Wesley with the permission of the publishers, Hinrichsen Edition Limited, London.

Father J. D. Crichton and The Quarterly of the Society of St. Gregory, for an extract from *Liturgy* (No. 151, July 1967).

The Revd. Dr. P. C. Moore, Vicar of Pershore Abbey, for permission to reproduce the photograph *The Living Liturgy*, taken by Mr. M. F. Couchman.

Mrs. E. V. Elliott, for assistance in the typing of this manuscript.

If we consider and ask ourselves what sort of music we should wish to hear on entering a church, we should surely, in describing our ideal, say first of all that it must be something different from what is heard from elsewhere; that it should be a sacred music, devoted to its purpose, a music whose peace should still passion, whose dignity should strengthen our faith, whose unquestioned beauty should find a home in our hearts, to cheer us in life and death; a music worthy of the fair temples in which we meet and of the holy words of our liturgy; a music whose expression of the mystery of things unseen never allowed any trifling motive to ruffle the sanctity of its reserve. What power for good such a music would have!

ROBERT BRIDGES [1]

By the voice of the celebrant and his ministers, and that of the people with their choir, the singing body of the assembly celebrates a festive liturgy which may be compared to a symphony. The voices indeed are divers, but the work is one. The Fathers of the Church loved to underline this unity in diversity, so characteristic of Christian worship. 'It is truly a great bond of union,' wrote St. Ambrose, 'that the multitude who form the assembly make us but one single chorus, just as the strings of the harp, though unequal in length, play harmoniously together. Even a skilled performer, playing on so few strings, may make a mistake; but in the liturgical singing of the community it is the Holy Spirit who is playing; from Him there is never any dissonance.' And St. John Chrysostom explains how the celebrating assembly can have but one voice: 'Because we all form one body together, there must be in the Church but one voice. Is it the reader who speaks? He does it alone; even the bishop who is present listens in silence. Is it the psalmist who chants? He chants alone; but when all reply to his chant, then it is as though but one voice were coming forth from one mouth.'

JOSEPH GELINEAU [2]

[1] *Collected Essays*, XXI–XXVI (Clarendon Press, 1935), page 65.
[2] *Voices and Instruments in Christian Worship* (Burns & Oates, 1964), page 73.

I. *The Beginnings of Music and Worship in England*

By the middle of the thirteenth century Salisbury Cathedral had become an important centre for the music and the performance of the Sarum Rite, due to the energetic reforms of Richard Poore (d. 1237). And Bishop Giles de Bridport writes:

> The church of Salisbury shines as the sun in its orb among the churches of the world in its divine service and those who minister in it, and by spreading its rays everywhere makes up for the defects of others.[1]

Many years of hard work and of liturgical experiment had effected this perfection. What do we know of the origins of liturgical music in England? and when were the first song schools established? What kind of music was actually performed in our monasteries and secular cathedrals? These are some of the questions that will be answered in this chapter.

It was a happy event in the history of English church music when Pope Gregory the Great sent Augustine, the Prior of St. Andrew's monastery in Rome, to refound the Catholic religion in this country. In 596 he set out with thirty-nine companions and eventually reached the shores of Kent in the summer of the following year. Augustine brought with him the Antiphoner and Missal of St. Gregory, as well as singers highly skilled in the Gregorian chant. And he also set about rebuilding the Cathedral Church of Christ in Canterbury, which by 630 possessed a flourishing song school.

[1] From *The Statutes and Customs of Salisbury*, page 88, quoted in Frank Ll. Harrison's *Music in Medieval Britain*, page 5.

B

Thus England began to absorb into its musical system the principles of the Gregorian monodic chant, even if certain differences in local methods of chanting hindered the idea of any musical uniformity in our churches. But with the arrival of Archbishop Theodore in 688, a uniformity of chanting was achieved:

> Being accompanied with the aforesaid Adrian (Abbot of St. Augustine's, Canterbury) he visited all the parts of this land. . . . Whereas before time there was in manner no singing in the English churches, except it were in Kent, now they began in every church to use singing of divine service after the rite of the Church of Rome.

Under the Normans there were instituted cathedral chapters of secular canons at Chichester, Exeter, Hereford, Lichfield, Lincoln, St. Paul's, Salisbury, Wells and York. These chapters comprised four dignitaries: Dean, Precentor, Chancellor and Treasurer. The Dean exercised complete control over the canons and priest-vicars. The Precentor (or *Primacerius,* i.e. the first name on the wax tablet recording the roll of singers) was the director of music and ceremonial; he also arranged the recitation of the Daily Hours, besides arranging the processions on festivals and the provision of music books for the choir. The Chancellor (*Magister scholarum*) had the oversight of the grammar schools and issued licences to all diocesan teachers; he drew up the canons' duty rota. The Treasurer was in charge of all the cathedral furnishings, sacred vessels, vestments, bells and lights. Sometimes he had an assistant, called a Sacrist.

Furthermore, the seating of a Norman cathedral consisted of three rows of benches—including return-stalls with their backs to the choir-screen, but facing east. The Dean and Sub-Dean sat on the south side of the choir (*decani*), nearest to the doors of the choir-screen; and the Precentor and the Succentor on the north side (*cantoris*). Also in the first row sat the Chancellor, the Treasurer, the Archdeacons and the numerous Priest-Vicars, who were responsible for the reading or singing of the services when their superiors were absent. The deacons and other clerks sat in the second row of benches on each side of the choir; and the choristers and probationers were placed in the front.

The special duties of reading and of singing were assigned weekly to either one side (*decani*) or the other (*cantoris*). And from the singers, certain rulers were appointed to sing particular parts of the liturgy and carried staves of office. They sang or read from one of the lecterns placed at the choir-step, in the middle of the choir, and on the choir-screen. The precentor was responsible for the list of singing duties, whereas the chancellor was in charge of the reading roster.

The Salisbury choristers were responsible for certain parts of the ceremonial. The seniors acted as thurifers and cross-bearers, and the juniors were taperers and holy-water bearers. Besides these important duties, the senior chorister had to read each week in the Chapter House as well as the first lesson at Mattins. Many of the boys served at the numerous altars. All this must have been very exacting, especially at great festivals which were marked by differences in cere-monial—lights, bells, vestments and processions.

The Franciscans

By 1224 the Franciscan Order was well established in England. Music was very much encouraged; and it was customary for the Brothers to sing one of the four votive-antiphons in honour of the Blessed Virgin after daily Com-pline. If the cities of Oxford and London were the intellectual *foci* of the Order, then the country towns and villages with their preaching crosses became fruitful ground for evangelistic activity: sermons, popular songs and carols formed the spiritual menu. And the friars interchanged the secular words of songs with religious ones, usually in the vernacular, hence the term *confractum* ('a parody of a secular song'). Richard de Ledrede, who was Bishop of Ossory, wrote Latin lyrics for the benefit of his junior clergy so that they should not 'pollute their throats by popular, immoral and secular songs.' His *Red Book of Ossory* (1317–60) included many refrains, equivalent to the English carol or *burden*. In fact, by the fifteenth century, carols were normally sung from Christmas until Epiphany in place of the *Benedicamus*.

The Rise of Choral Foundations and Song Schools

These foundations have played an important part in Anglican worship and religious education. The Chapel Royal was modelled upon the Sainte-Chapelle at Paris, which had been built by Louis IX in 1245 to house the Crown of Thorns and other relics of the Passion. By 1299 this Chapel's staff consisted of thirteen canons, thirteen priest-chaplains, thirteen clerk-deacons and six choirboys, who were supervised by the *maitrise*. But the English Chapel Royal was composed of chaplains and clerks, whose main duties were to assist the king in his private devotions, to say Mass daily for the household and to hear their confessions. Whenever the king travelled abroad, the Chapel staff was in constant attendance. And we know that the Master of the Children, John Pyamour, was authorized in 1420 to press-gang choirboys from other choirs, so that they could be taken with him to Normandy where King Henry V was staying.

In 1483 King Edward III incorporated the Royal Free Chapel of the Household, which consisted of a dean, three canons, twenty-four chaplains and clerks, eight choirboys and one Master of the Children, who was apparently appointed by the dean from one of the Gentlemen of the Chapel. And the Children of the Chapel were well cared for, being boarded in the royal palace and possessing special privileges. They were later given a distinctive uniform of elaborate red-and-gold coats, which are still worn to-day.

Many of our educational foundations had fine choirs due to the individual interest of bishops and kings. William of Wykeham, Bishop of Winchester, had provided for three lay-clerks and sixteen choirboys to sing the daily offices both at New College and at Winchester, where the boys had to be under twelve years old, skilled in reading and singing, as well as having to make the beds of the residential Fellows! Another Bishop of Winchester, William Wayneflete, was equally beneficent in founding Magdalen College, Oxford, whose choir contained eight lay-clerks and sixteen choristers. King Henry VI himself founded the two famous Colleges of Our Lady at Eton and at Cambridge (1440–1), which both had a provost, ten fellows, ten chaplains, ten lay-clerks and sixteen choristers—mostly drawn from the choirs of Salisbury and Norwich.

The rise of separate choirs for lay-clerks and boys was due more than anything else to the increased medieval devotion to our Lady, which required the singing of extra votive masses and antiphons. By 1225, there was a daily celebration of the Lady Mass in the Lady Chapel at Salisbury Cathedral, which was sung by four lay-clerks and several choristers. And Bishop Alcock endowed the Lady Chapel at Worcester in 1478 for the maintenance of a master, clerks and choristers. Another important duty of the Lady Chapel choir was the singing of the evening antiphon in honour of our Lady at the end of Compline.

Choristers themselves lived at first in the canons' houses and acted as their domestic servants in return for their board and lodging. In 1264, however, Bishop Richard de Gravesend authorized that the Lincoln choirboys were to be housed under one roof and to be supervised by one master. And it was natural for the Dean of Lincoln, Roger de Montival, to facilitate the same reforms at Salisbury when he was appointed to its See, because he observed that the choristers were being drawn into walking round the canons' houses 'to crave a beggar's dole each day.' And so he appointed one of the canons to act as their warden or *custos*.

Most of our cathedral choirs averaged about twelve choristers at this time. And some establishments went through troubled moments due to the bad behaviour of the lay-clerks. Bishop Beauchamp, for instance, reported that three of the Salisbury lay-clerks were frequently running off into the town to play tennis and to go to the taverns, where they sat drinking and singing. This resulted in the more conscientious singers entering into royal service, where there were higher standards of singing and the prospects of better stipends.

The Organum

The thirteenth century saw the birth of organized polyphony in Western music. We know that the organ was first introduced into France from Constantinople towards the end of the eighth century and that polyphony originated from the East. Therefore it is likely that the simultaneous sounding of separate notes upon this instrument by two organ-strikers may have afforded singers the same incentive. In most parish churches the listener experiences *organum,* or harmonized music, when male voices unwittingly sing an octave below the treble line and the unmusically inclined invariably drone a fourth below. *Organum* involves the organizing of parts as a means of variety to the plainsong melody, which is usually given to the tenor (Latin, *tenere* = 'to hold'). And with the tenor's holding on to the plainsong melody, the other voices sang the same tune an octave, or a fifth, or a fourth, below. But, whenever the voices sang together homophonically, a rich sonorous sound came forth (*bassus*). Another method of this type of singing is called 'free descant' because the lower parts are transferred above the tenor, thus forming second and third parts; both these methods could be done by ear or by improvisation. An early example of this 'free *organum*' is recorded at Romsey Abbey in 991: 'While the *decani* side of the choir sang a melodious strain with excellent voices, the *cantoris* side laboured at *organum* parts in jubilant songs of praise.' Moreover, Gerald de Barri (*c.* 1147–1220) refers to the Welsh practice of free improvisation and to the Yorkshireman, who harmonized in two parts: 'one murmuring below, the other soothing and charming the ear above.' The English delighted in two-part singing, wherein they employed consecutive thirds which was later called *gymel,* or twin-song.

The Conductus and Motet

The *conductus* is essentially 'a song for ceremonial procession,' which had fixed or more simplified rhythms; otherwise the procession would have been chaotic. It was sung in the Mass when one of the ministers wished to move in order to carry out a particular function, for example, the reading of the Epistle and the singing of the Gospel. The verse required to be of a uniform length, and the same melody was sung for each one by the lowest voice. The upper voices merely vocalized a vowel-sound from the liturgical text.

The *motet* made its appearance in the Ordinary of the Mass, the Magnificats and the Antiphons. It was sung by singers who were stationed at a lectern, placed in the middle of the choir and facing the altar. The motet was a development of the *clausula,* which was a short plainsong phrase that could be repeated several times. Thus, by adding words to the upper parts the *clausula* grew into a motet. In its simplest form, the motet consisted of a lower part (*tenor*) and an upper part (*motetus,* from the French word *mot*). And sometimes an instrument was used to reinforce the *tenor*; thus it was not long before three parts were formed with the treble (*triplum*) placed above the *motetus.*

Many motets were polytextual. The simplest form consisted of the *tenor* part with two upper parts singing an identical text, so creating a trope upon the liturgical text of the *tenor*. But the term 'double motet' was used wherever the two upper voices sang different texts. In France particularly, a variety was achieved by using the texts of love songs in the *triplum* and the liturgical text in the *motetus*. Needless to say, this custom was severely condemned by the church authorities because they disliked the heart of the sacred liturgy being corrupted by the secular. However, the appearance of the bi-lingual motet was a passing one, affording yet another example of the sacred and the secular existing alongside in church music. In the words of Manfred Bukofzer:

It must be emphasized that the sacred and secular

spheres overlapped to a considerable degree, and that the contrast between secular and sacred music was not as absolute as has often been claimed. It is extremely difficult, if not impossible, to give an *a priori* definition of sacred and secular style in music and to determine on this basis in what way the one may have affected the other. The distinction of secular and sacred is essentially one of musical function, not of musical style.[2]

With the rise of the *Ars Nova* (*c*. 1310–*c*. 1435), the motet underwent a renaissance. The name *Ars Nova* was borrowed from Philippe de Vitry's book (1320) and referred to the introduction of a new system of motet writing wherein a greater variety of notation was used: breves, semi-breves and minims. Another breakthrough came with the advent of *isorhythm*, that is to say, the variation of a given melody by setting it to different rhythms. The basic rhythmical pattern was called the *talea*, and the melodic decoration was termed the *color*, a medieval rhetorical term referring to any kind of repetition.

Hockets, or rests, were utilized in certain rhythms, which was a secular device 'more at home in the hall than in the church, where its employment was soundly rebuked at times by the bishops and other writers' (Dom Anselm Hughes). No wonder, hockets were derived from the French hunting songs; and even the Puritan John Wycliffe remarked in one of his sermons that three or four proud rascals in a choir would often sing the service with flourishes so that nobody could hear the words: all the others were dumb and watched them like fools! Another critic was John of Salisbury (*c*. 1115–80), who confirmed that the religious music of his day defiled the services 'by the riot of the wantoning voice, by its eager ostentation, and by female affectations in the mincing of notes and cadences.'

Moreover, the use of duple-time also featured in the composition of motets during this period.

[2] From *The New Oxford History of Music*, Vol. III, page 107.

Composers

LEONEL POWER (d. 1445), probably the Master of the Choristers at Canterbury Cathedral, was one of the most distinguished lay-clerks in England. He was influenced by the medieval devotion to the Virgin Mary in whose honour he composed fifteen motets. Power himself contributed to the unification of the Ordinary of the Mass by borrowing an existing plainsong melody and then using it throughout the various sections—hence creating the cyclic-tenor Mass, of which his *Alma redemptoris mater* (1430) is one of the earliest examples. And he followed the English custom of not setting the *Kyries* to music, as well as reducing the voices both in the *Pleni sunt coeli* and the *Benedictus qui venit* of the *Sanctus*. He achieves considerable contrast in his music by giving sections for full choir, as well as duets for solo voices.

JOHN DUNSTABLE (*c.* 1390–1453), an international figure among church musicians, was a talented astrologer and mathematician. He was also a member of the private chapel of John, Duke of Bedford, and an absentee canon of Hereford Cathedral between the years 1419 and 1440.

Dunstable was a master at melodic paraphrase. He avoided the dissonant styles of the previous century by writing smoother progressions. And he delighted in using major and minor triads. But this must not infer that he was unable to write more complex works; compare, for example, the isorhythmic technique in the Motet, *Veni, Sancte Spiritus* (H). And he preferred to write in more flexible rhythms than in the rigid style of the *conductus,* which is seen in the flowing melodies of *Regina caeli laetare* (BP) and *Quam pulchra es* (SB). Dunstable's other compositions include the Mass *Rex Seculorum* (SB) and the Magnificat in the Second Tone (SB), as well as the Motet *Sancta Maria* (SB).

ROBERT FAYRFAX (1464–1521), the organist at St. Albans Abbey, was a Gentleman of the Chapel Royal and Composer to the Royal Household. He was accounted 'the prime musician of the nation' and is the earliest recorded to have attained the Oxford D.Mus. (1511); and he also directed the English choir in the ceremonies at the Cloth of Gold (1520). Although his music is written in an imitative style, it avoids the florid harmonizations and ornamented melodies of contemporary works. Fayrfax wrote five Festal Masses and the *Magnificat Regale* (SB), wherein are sections for duets, trios and quartets.

WILLIAM CORNYSH (*c.* 1465–1523) was a gifted playwright and a personal friend of King Henry VIII. He came from a musical family; in fact his eldest brother is the earliest named Master of the Song School at Westminster Abbey (1479). 'William Cornysh Junior,' as he came to be called, was appointed Master of the Children (1509–23) and had the curious job of supplying paving-stones, sanitary equipment and guttering to the Court. Although none of his Masses have survived, some of his Motets fortunately have—such as the floridly-written *Stabat Mater* and the simply-constructed *Ave Maria mater Dei* (SB). And there is a beautiful setting of the Passiontide Carol, *Woefully arrayed*.

JOHN TAVERNER (*c.* 1495–1545) was first employed as a lay-clerk at the collegiate church of Tattershall in Boston. Afterwards he was made the first *informator* at Cardinal College, Oxford, where he was forced into writing new music for its Chapel (later Christ Church Cathedral), that included five Shorter Masses and three Festal Settings: *Corona Spinea, O Michael* and *Gloria tibi Trinitas* (SB).

The best known of his five Shorter Masses is undoubtedly *The Western Wynde* (SB), which is 'a parody Mass' founded upon a secular tune that occurs thirty-six times in the work. Taverner's liturgical music is written in a forceful Flemish style, but with little sensitivity shown towards their texts. A variety of musical texture is evident in the use of antiphony, homophony and polyphony in the vocal writing. He has composed, too, three settings of the Magnificat and a five-part setting of the Te Deum.

The Architectural Setting of Worship

The choir served as the private chapel of the monks and was an enclosed compartment, occupying almost two-thirds of the entire building. In many cases, the stone *pulpitum* was all that the congregation would have seen, for example: Ripon, Southwell and York Minster. And where it had been situated at the east end of the nave, the *pulpitum* was brought farther back into the choir, thus leaving the crossing and the transepts free for public worship and processions, which had been successfully achieved at Wells. And one of the results of the Mariolatry Cult, fostered by Pope Innocent III (d. 1216), was the erection of new Lady Chapels at the eastern arm of our retro-choirs as can be seen at Chichester, Salisbury and Exeter. Special services for the laity were held here, in which the clergy were assisted by a choir of lay-clerks and boys.

Conclusion

The musical menu of the medieval church was a varied and exciting one. Choirs were not large and could be compared to a small chamber orchestra, where the lay-clerks were the soloists. Moreover, the High Mass with its elaborate ceremonial and festive music was undoubtedly a splendid occasion; even the lessons at the Offices were sung to polyphonic music at the greater feasts. The English antiphon, from which the term 'anthem' has been derived, was modelled upon the Mary-antiphons sung after Compline. And the Shorter Masses were written for the Lady Chapel choir, but including this time settings of the *Kyries* with alternating sections for plainsong and polyphony. The *chanson* style in French liturgical music was gradually assimilated within English church music at the end of the fourteenth century.

If church architecture was embellished with slender pillars and beautifully carved capitals as to be found in the Chapter House at Southwell Minster, so liturgical music was equally embellished with graceful flourishes or *melismas,* particularly in the polyphonic music of the Festal Mass and Magnificat.

Yet there were many critics of this spirited decoration in sacred music, who held that the *Ars Nova* movement had acted as a magic spell by intoxicating the ears and by benumbing the souls of church musicians. And from the battlements of Avignon, Pope John XXII issued the encyclical *Docta sanctorum Patrum* (1324–5) which advocated an immediate return to the simplicity of the Gregorian Chant and condemned those singers, 'who truncate the melodies with hockets, deprave them with descants, and even trope the upper parts with secular songs.' And even priests were commanded to sing their services reverently to suitable music, as well as to delight in good enunciation. The basic problem was whether the Church should choose between the sacred and the secular in liturgical music, or should effect a compromise but with adequate safeguards? An example of such a compromise is the Canon, *Sumer is icumen* (*c.* 1270), that is also set to the sacred text, *Perspice christicola* ('Look, O worshipper of Christ').

II. *The Reformation and Edwardine Church Music*

The sixteenth century was an age of renewal, witnessing liturgical and doctrinal reforms not only in England, but on the Continent, especially in Germany and Switzerland. A Dutch scholar, Erasmus of Rotterdam, had many scathing things to say against the institution of the Church; and he felt that too much time had been wasted on church music:

> They chant nowadays in our churches in what is an unknown tongue and nothing else, while you will not hear a sermon once in six months telling people to amend their lives. Modern church music is so constructed that the congregation cannot hear a single word clearly, and the choristers themselves do not understand what they are singing.[1]

The Reformers supported the use of secular tunes in the musical parts of the divine service. Luther himself had grown up from childhood to appreciate music in worship, especially the old German carols and sacred songs. And he was reputed to have remarked, 'The devil does not need all the good tunes for himself!' Although he had no objection to professional choirs, he preferred the sound of hearty, congregational singing and of religious songs in homes. And he once wrote to a personal friend:

> It is my intention to make German psalms for the people, spiritual songs whereby the Word of God may be kept alive in them by singing. . . . I desire that new-fangled and courtly expressions may be avoided and that the words may all be exceedingly simple and common, such as plain folk may understand.

[1] From his *Commentary to the New Testament*, viz. 1 Cor. 14:19.

The intelligibility of the sacred text was of most importance. Even Pope Marcellus II had to summon the Papal choir into his presence in 1550, when he impressed upon the singers that the mysteries of the Passion were to be sung in a suitable manner, with modulated voices so that everything could be both heard and understood. At the Council of Trent, a commission of cardinals reported to Pope Paul IV about the main principles of Roman Catholic church music, particularly in the musical settings of the Mass:

> Let nothing profane be intermingled, but only hymns and divine praises. The singing should be arranged not only to give empty pleasure to the ear, but in such a way that the words may be clearly understood by all, and thus the hearts of the listeners be drawn to the desire of the heavenly harmonies, in the contemplation of the joys of the blessed.[2]

The English Reformation began as a political manœuvre on the part of King Henry VIII, who had an intense dislike to the church courts and our canon law being subjected to the ruling of the Papacy. And in 1534 the King was appointed as 'the Supreme Head of the Church of England,' with the added powers 'to reform all errors, heresies and abuses in the same.' Four years later he commanded Becket's tomb in Canterbury Cathedral to be desecrated. To the staunch ardent Catholics this was nothing less than an act of sacrilege; but to the nationalists it was a symbol of their liberation from the shackles of Roman Catholicism.

At this time there was also a questioning of biblical and doctrinal beliefs by our scholars. In Cambridge, for instance, the Franciscans Robert Barnes and Miles Coverdale were holding private discussions in the White Horse Tavern, together with Thomas Bilney, Hugh Latimer and two future Archbishops, Thomas Cranmer and Matthew Parker. They were particularly interested in the new theological ideas

[2] From *Music in the Renaissance* by Gustave Reese (Dent, 1959), page 449.

being taught by Martin Luther of Wittenberg. And it was Thomas Starkey, the King's Chaplain, who desired that the liturgy should be said in the vernacular. But the King was still very conservative in religious matters and forbade the innovation. Nevertheless, Convocation petitioned him for an authoritative translation of the Scriptures; and in 1536 both English and Latin Bibles were placed in our churches, 'for every man that will to look and read thereon.' Again, the Royal Injunction of 1538 commanded 'the Bible in the largest volume in English' to be placed in churches throughout the land. Yet the more conservative members of the Church regarded this action with disdain: 'I never read the Scriptures, nor never will read it,' retorted the Catholic Duke of Norfolk; 'it was merry England afore the New Learning came up—yea, I would all things were as hath been in the past.'

The years 1536–40 witnessed the dissolution of the monasteries. The last one to surrender peaceably was Waltham Abbey, where Thomas Tallis was the director of music. With this unfortunate action went the hanging of several abbots, the dispersion of valuable music libraries and the closing of many song schools. Although the disbanding of these choirs and the closure of these schools might seem a tragedy for English church music, it did result in the dispersion of singers throughout the country, whose singing later enriched the secular music of the private households in Elizabeth's reign. But there were exceptions in many churches and chapels, because under both the Old and the New Foundations there were still paid singers; and many deans were the former abbots of their respective churches. For example, the Constitution of 1540 created Westminster Abbey into a Collegiate Church under the authority of Dean (Abbot) Boston and twelve prebendaries. The rest of the new establishment consisted of twelve lay-clerks, ten choirboys, the choirmaster, a gospeller and epistoller.

The Place of Music in Worship

The opinions of the English reformers differed over the

use of music in public worship. Whereas most people liked having some music in the services, the extremists hated it in any form. However, the *Book of Ceremonies* (1539) was more favourable towards church music:

> The sober, discreet and devout singing music and playing with organs, used in church in the service of God, are ordained to move and stir the people to the sweetness of God's Word, the which is there sung: and by that sweet harmony both to excite them to prayer and devotion, and also to put them in remembrance of the heavenly triumphant Church, where is everlasting joy and praise to God.

And the findings of the Council of Trent on church music, especially in their emphasis upon the intelligibility of the liturgical text, were expressed earlier by the Royal Injunction to the Dean and Chapter of Lincoln in April of 1548, namely:

> They shall from henceforth sing and say no anthems of our Lady or other Saints, but only of our Lord, and them not in Latin; but choosing out the best and most sounding to Christian religion they shall turn the same into English, setting thereunto a plain and distinct note for every syllable one: they shall sing them and none other.

The English Litany

Because of a serious failure in the crops during 1544, the King commanded that processions with prayers should be held throughout the land. These proved unpopular with the ordinary people who were accustomed to having prayers said in the Latin tongue. However, in June, when England was 'plagued with most cruel wars' against both France and Scotland, the Archbishop was authorized to issue 'in our native English tongue, the Litany with suffrages to be sung in time of processions.' Cranmer had ingeniously adapted the Latin plainsong tones to the English text, and the music became immediately familiar to the people. And in a letter addressed to the King, he wrote:

> In mine opinion, the song that shall be made thereunto would not be full of notes, but, as near as may be, for every syllable a note; so that it may be sung distinctly and devoutly, as be in Mattins and Evensong *Venite*, the hymns *Te Deum, Benedictus, Magnificat, Nunc Dimittis* and all the Psalms and Versicles; and in the mass *Gloria in excelsis, Gloria Patri*, the Creed, the Preface, the *Pater Noster* and some of the *Sanctus* and *Agnus*. . . . Nevertheless, they that be cunning in singing can make a much more solemn note thereto. I made them only for a proof to see how the English would do in song.

Whereas some composers endeavoured to keep to this note-against-note style, which had in some way been effected in Taverner's *Playn Song* Mass, the sixteenth century composers disregarded it and wrote Great Services, which contained melismatic flourishes and much verbal repetition.

The Edwardine Reforms

In February 1547, the nine-year-old King Edward VI was crowned in Westminster Abbey. The English Reformation was now in the hands of his advisers, who sincerely believed that the King's main duty was to complete whatever liturgical reforms his father had failed to achieve. In fact, the congregation's right to participate in public worship was given special attention. By April, an English form of Compline was sung in the Chapel Royal. And in the following September the Epistles and Gospels were permitted to be read in the vernacular, together with the Ordinary of the Mass at the November Service for the opening of both Convocation and Parliament. The services of Mattins and Evensong had already been sung in St. Paul's Cathedral and many other churches. But the extreme Reformers disliked Latin polyphonic music—only anthems of our Lord, with English texts and plainly sung music, were allowed in worship.

The Book of Common Prayer

This was first published by Edward Whitchurch on March 7th, 1549. The Book was both scriptural and didactic because men needed to be edified, which involved the building up of their souls for eternal life (e.g. the *Exhortations*). Cranmer's ideal is well expressed in the text, 'Thy word is a lantern unto my feet' (Psalm 119), since the continual reading of the Bible was the basic pattern of all Protestant worship. This return to the Scriptures resulted in many of the musical sections of the English liturgy being drastically pruned: 'For this cause be cut of Anthems, Responds, Invitatories, and such like things as did break the continual course of the reading of the scripture.' And there were inserted many rubrics directing what liturgical vesture was to be worn and what ceremonies were to be retained, because 'they have much blinded the people and obscured the glory of God.' Moreover, it was specified what attitude should be adopted in the conduct of worship: 'As touching kneeling, crossing, holding up of hands, knocking upon the breast, and other gestures: they may be used or left as every man's devotion serveth without blame.'

The Book of Common Prayer was in the vernacular and, together with the Bible, was to be the only Use throughout the country. Much stress was placed upon congregational participation. People were no longer allowed to be dumb or to be left in the aisles saying their private prayers. Every person had to join with the clerks in the singing of the Creed and in the saying of the Lord's Prayer, besides taking an active part in the Versicles and Responses. Although this First Book was a conservative revision of the Sarum Rite, there were several doctrinal omissions, such as the existence of purgatory and the invocation of the saints.

Clear directives indicated what parts of these Services were to be either said or sung. Most of the liturgy in the village churches was said, although in our cathedrals and collegiate churches the term *said* would have implied a simple intonation, and the term *sung* would have meant a more elaborate setting. After the Venite came this rubric:

> Then shall follow certain Psalms in order as they have been appointed in a table made for the purpose, except there be Proper Psalms appointed for that day. And at the end of every Psalm, Magnificat, and Nunc Dimittis, shall be repeated: Glory be to the Father and to the Son, etc.

Moreover, the Act of Uniformity had previously authorized the use of any Psalms taken from the Bible, 'not letting or omitting thereby the service or any part thereof mentioned in the said book.' The Psalms followed a monthly cycle. And in most churches the congregation would have repeated the words of each verse after the clerk, who read them from his personal copy of the Scriptures. Hence arose the custom of *lining-out*.

Although the Psalter was not printed with *The Book of Common Prayer* until 1662, there was issued *The Psalter, corrected and pointed as the Psalms shall be sung in churches after the translation of the Great Bible* (1549). Such a book must have been a god-send to our congregations because it contained the days of the month 'titled over the head of the leaf,' together with the sections for Morning and Evening Prayer clearly indicated in the text. Concerning what music was used in the singing of these Psalms, Dr. Lamb writes:

> Before the Reformation, they were chanted in plainsong, not by the congregation, but by the priest and choir. Everywhere the reformers sought to bring in a more corporate understanding and rendering of the services, and in England it was the intention that all should 'sing or say' the psalms. The difficulty was that few could read words, and perhaps fewer still could read music. However it seems that when the Prayer Book was issued, the psalms would be sung to some modification of the plainsong tones. This might have been difficult to arrange, considering the differences between Latin and English speech. But that some adjustment was made is suggested by the work of Merbecke.

Though there are no completely noted psalms, we have his music for the canticles and also the opening verse of Psalm 1 pointed for the Introits at Holy Communion. These were all unaccompanied, but before long composers prepared settings in harmony, and these were suited only to choirs, especially those of cathedrals. It may have been this difficulty about congregational singing that led to the wide popularity of the metrical psalter.[3]

The responsibility for reading and intoning the Lessons, as well as for the other parts of the services, was given to the Priest-Vicar, who was a Minor Canon. And, if there were no priests or deacons available, a lay-clerk was called in to assist. In the Chapel Royal a special position of *Pistoler* was held by two laymen. Whether a Lesson was said or sung depended entirely upon local circumstances, which is supported by this rubric directing how the Lessons were to be rendered:

> And to the end the people may better hear in such places where they do sing, there shall the Lessons be sung in a plain tune after the manner of distinct reading: and likewise the Epistle and Gospel.

Both the *Te Deum* and the *Benedictus* were sung throughout the year, except when the former was replaced by the *Benedicite* in Lent. And Evensong followed the liturgical pattern of Mattins.

There were appended two rubrics to the Eucharist authorizing the use of the Litany on Wednesdays and Fridays and that the priest should say all parts of the Communion Service in places where there were no singers available. Composers were encouraged to write new music for the English Rite. At the request of Archbishop Cranmer, John Merbecke produced *The booke of Common praier noted* (1550). But

[3] From *The Psalms in Christian Worship* (Faith Press, 1962), pages 148–9.

its life was cut short due to the publication of *The Book of Common Prayer* (1552) which involved too many changes in order to accommodate the liturgical text.

An Act of Parliament empowered King Edward VI to appoint a commission to draft *The English Ordinal,* which was later published in March of 1550. Its music was cut down to a minimum, comprising the singing of the Litany and *Veni Creator.* However, one of three Proper Psalms could be sung as an Introit at the Communion Service for the Ordination of Priests.

The Second English Prayer Book

The First Book of Common Prayer (1549) was a moderate revision of the Sarum Rite; hence the Archbishop's remarks to the Cornish rebels : 'It seemeth to you a new service, and indeed it is none other than the old; the self-same in English which were in Latin, saving a few things taken out.' Thus, it was not in the least surprising that the Catholic-minded clergy continued in their ritualistic practices, making a radical Bishop like John Hooper of Gloucester write :

> I am so much offended with that book, and that not without abundant reason, that if it be not corrected, I neither can nor will communicate with the Church in the Administration of the Supper.

And the *Censura* (1551) of the Regius Professor of Divinity at Cambridge, Martin Bucer, contained many chapters against ritualistic practices and the saying of prayers for the departed that were not sanctioned by the first Book. Further, he wrote strongly concerning the correct position of the choir in worship :

> For, that the choir should be so distantly separated from the rest of the temple, and the service (which pertains to the whole people and the clergy) be set forth in it alone, is anti-Christian. So great a separation of the choir from the rest of the temple serves to this end,

37

that the ministers (of whatsoever faith and life they be) are yet by their order and position considered as nearer to God than lay people, and able to make God propitious to them by means of external works, which they reserve to themselves, though they belong to the whole people of Christ: and also because the performance of those public services in the choir alone confirms the pernicious superstition by which reading, reciting and hearing the Scriptures and prayers, without intelligence and without the understanding of faith, is thought a worship pleasing to God. . . . From the plans of the most ancient temples, and from the writings of the holy fathers, it is well known that among the ancients the position of the clergy was in the middle of the temples, which were usually round: and from that position divine service was so presented to the people that the things recited could be clearly heard and understood by all who were present.[4]

This *Second English Book of Common Prayer* (1552) was drafted by the Windsor Commission, but without the approval of the Convocations. The Boy-King was entirely in the hands of the Council, especially of his uncle the Duke of Northumberland, who was the champion of the left-wing reforming party that taught a Swiss doctrine of the Eucharist. This Book became our equivalent of John Knox's *Genevan Service Book* (1556).

When the new liturgy was first used in St. Paul's Cathedral on All Saints' Day 1552 the choir was dispersed, the organ silenced, and the officiants, according to the directions of a new rubric, wore neither alb, vestment, nor cope. Protestantism was enthroned in all its starkness at the heart of England's religious life.[5]

[4] From *The Architectural Setting of Anglican Worship* (Faber & Faber, 1948), pages 245–6.
[5] From C. M. Ady's *The English Church* (Faber & Faber, 1940), page 178.

How this change in vesture affected English Church Music will be discussed in another chapter. In the Eucharist, the Introit, *Benedictus, Agnus Dei* and the Communion Proper were cut from the Service. And in the place of the Ninefold Kyries was inserted the Decalogue. The Gloria was retained, but now sung before the Blessing. The Creed was said, thus cutting down the musical parts of the Service to a minimum. Some drastic changes came in the Canon, with the omission of both the *Epiklesis* and the *Anamnesis* as well as the transference of the Communion Devotions to before the *Sursum Corda*. The phrase, *in these Holy Mysteries* was deleted from the Prayer of Humble Access. And the Words of Administration emphasized a mere remembrance of Christ's Passion with the individual soul's 'feeding upon Him by faith with thanksgiving.' The Black Rubric was inserted without Parliamentary authority; and the priest now stood at the north side of the table, which was placed in the centre of the choir.

The structure of the Daily Offices was in sympathy with the liturgical principles of the reformers, comprising the People's Preparation (Scriptural Sentences, Exhortation, Confession and Absolution), God's Word to His people (Lessons, Canticles and Sermon) and finally their Response. Flexibility was evident in its alternatives: *Benedicite* for *Te Deum, Jubilate* (Psalm 100) for *Benedictus, Cantate Domino* (Psalm 98) for *Magnificat, Deus Misereatur* (Psalm 67) for *Nunc Dimittis,* and the *Quicunque vult* to be said or sung after *Benedictus.*

The Characteristics of Edwardine Church Music

There was a considerable variety of musical texture, ranging from the plain-song simplicity of Merbecke's *Communion Service* to the more complex and contrapuntal music of Tallis's *Spem in alium*. And in between came the homophonic music of Tallis's *Festal Psalms,* similar to the future Anglican Chants. Whereas in the past the composers achieved variety through descants and *canti firmi,* resulting in a coarser tone, the Tudor composers created a polyphonic

39

technique that grew into one of the glories of English Church Music—no wonder an Italian visitor to the Chapel Royal in 1515 exclaimed that the children's singing was more divine than human! Composers of this period were always being tempted into writing elaborate music for the liturgy; hence were born the *Great Services* of Byrd and Gibbons.[6]

Nevertheless, Cranmer's principle of a note for every syllable did see the simplification of part-writing and the emergence of the *Short Services.* The Edwardine period marked a cessation in the writing of motets in honour of the Virgin, due more than anything else to the prevalent anti-Marian feeling among the English Reformers. Composers took care that the *Gloria, Credo, Sanctus* and *Agnus Dei* were of equal length. But very few composers utilized existing secular melodies in writing new music for the Mass, with the exception of the well-known tune (*The Western Wynde*). Furthermore, the polyphonic setting of the Nine-fold Kyrie proved unpopular since it required too much time and delayed the liturgical action. A compromise was made in certain cases through *alternatim* settings that combined both plainsong and polyphony. By 1552 the Kyrie had dropped its three sections and had become a response to the Decalogue.

The motet formed an essential part of the musical menu of the Sarum Rite. Neither frequent modulation nor bar-lines were employed at this stage. The glory of these motets lies in their unaccompanied flowing parts, which reached a climax at the final phrase of the music: hence a uniform cadence is achieved through words and music coming together. And nowhere is this more apparent than in the final *Amens* of the *Great Services* of the Tudor period.

The middle of the sixteenth century saw the birth of metrical psalmody in England. It was a Member of Parliament for Plymouth and one of the grooms of the Royal Wardrobe, Thomas Sternhold, who wrote nineteen such para-

[6] Technique for the sixteenth century composer was the method of expressing his thought or the writer's thought. Consult H. K. Andrews, *The Technique of Byrd's Vocal Polyphony* (OUP, 1966), for an extensive treatment of this subject.

phrases entitled *Certayne Psalmes, chosen out of the Psalter of David and drawen into English metre* (1547). And it was the young Edward VI who encouraged him to publish these new settings of the Psalms for the enjoyment of others. This edition was dedicated to the King, and was followed by another one containing thirty-seven psalms in 1549. The third edition (1557) contained seven more psalms by a Suffolk clergyman and schoolmaster, John Hopkins.

The immediate popularity of what became known as 'Sternhold and Hopkins' was due to the verses being written in English ballad metre.

The Composers of the Age

It is necessary to emphasize that the Tudor composers were born into the life of the Catholic Church. Many of them had been Children of the Chapel Royal, thus gaining an excellent knowledge of the liturgy. They indeed experienced and lived the life of the contemporary Church. All great church music has been written within the spiritual climate of the worshipping community and must therefore become the handmaid of the liturgical text.

CHRISTOPHER TYE (*c.* 1505–1572) was appointed in 1542 Master of the Choristers at Ely Cathedral where he remained for nineteen years. He wrote three Masses and a setting of the Evening Canticles (OUP). He also translated fourteen chapters from the *Acts of the Apostles* in 1553, the music of which he dedicated to the Boy-King, Edward VI, in appreciation for having been appointed Music Master to the Royal Family. The motets are characteristic for their simplicity and introduce something new to English Church Music by having the melody placed in the treble, instead of the tenor.

Motets:

Christ rising again	OUP
Give alms of thy goods	OUP
Hail, glorious spirits	RSCM
O come, ye servants of the Lord	RSCM

O God of Bethel	OUP
O Holy Spirit, Lord of Grace	RSCM
Omnes gentes plaudite	CH
Rubum quem viderat Moyses	CH
The eternal gates lift up their heads	RSCM
Once, only once	RSCM

THOMAS TALLIS (1505–85) has been appropriately called 'our Palestrina,' because his liturgical music was set to Latin texts. In 1531 he was the organist of Dover Priory, and afterwards he sang for six years in one of London's City churches. And in the summer of 1538 he was appointed the organist of Waltham Abbey, where he remained until 1540. He has the distinction of serving under four English monarchs, in spite of his strong Catholic sympathies. Queen Elizabeth displayed her kindness by granting to both Tallis and William Byrd a monopoly for printing music and manuscript paper from 1574 until 1585. Both Tallis and Byrd were joint-organists at the Chapel Royal. They published *Cantiones quae ab argumento sacrae vocantur* (1575), a collection of Latin motets dedicated to Queen Elizabeth in appreciation of the monopoly that she had given to them. Each composer contributed seventeen motets, corresponding to the seventeen years during which she had reigned. By this time Thomas Tallis was an old man of seventy. His well-known setting, *Salvator Mundi* (OUP) first appeared in this book.

Before the year 1552 Tallis wrote three sets of *Festal Psalms* for the Evenings of Christmas Eve, Christmas Day and St. Stephen's Day, which were a novelty because it was usual for the psalms to be sung to plainsong. And in Archbishop Parker's *Whole Psalter* (1567) came eight of his tunes, including the famous *Canon* composed for Psalm 67. It was later set to Evening Hymn (AMR 23), which Bishop Ken had written for Winchester College in 1692. Tallis's *Ordinal* (AMR 545) was inserted into the Archbishop's Psalter as an extra tune. He also composed many hymns for alternating plainsong and polyphony: a method outlined in many of the medieval service books.

There is a distinct brightness about his motets, which is especially seen in *Salvator Mundi*. But there exists one extended work which is an exception: *The Lamentations of Jeremiah the Prophet* (OUP) with its text derived from the first Nocturn of Maundy Thursday. Here, there is no place for the brightness of boys' voices, but only for the contemplative polyphony of the men's voices. The climax occurs in the middle of Part One, when the lower parts imitate in chordal form the sopranos' pathetic utterances of *Jerusalem, Jerusalem, convertere ad Dominum Deum tuum*. Undoubtedly Tallis reaches the height of his powers in the celebrated forty-part Motet, *Spem in alium non habui* (OUP), wherein a majestic pattern of thematic material is blended into a powerful unity. An organ part has recently been discovered, which is unique because it was only customary for the organ in Tallis's time to insert interludes between the verses of hymns, as in his plainsong setting *Ecce tempus idoneum* where the plainsong motifs are repeated by the organ as a solo.

Tallis also composed two *Short Services* (OUP) that comply with the Cranmerian ideal of 'one note to a syllable.' He arranged a popular setting of the *Preces and Responses* (CMS) and the *Litany for Five Voices* (FP).

WILLIAM MUNDY (*c.* 1530–91) was a Gentleman of the Chapel Royal, although a practising Roman Catholic. He wrote music both for the Roman and English Rites. Many of his compositions are devotional in character, e.g. *Ah helpless wretch* (BP), which appeared in a collection compiled by the Master of the Children, William Hunnis. Together with Richard Farrant and William Byrd, he has the distinction of writing some of the earliest verse anthems in English Church Music. He wrote a *Complete Service* (N) and the well-known anthem, *O Lord the Maker of all things* (OUP), set to words from *The King's Primer* (1545).

RICHARD FARRANT (before 1535–81) worked alongside John Merbecke and was finally appointed the organist and master of the choristers at St. George's Chapel, Windsor, in 1564. Much of his time was spent in the writing of incidental music for secular plays, which he produced with the choristers, and thus accounted for the small output of church music from his hand. He did write a Morning and Evening Service in A Minor (OUP), which is marked by its simplicity of style, and many anthems including *Call to remembrance* (OUP), *Hide not thy face* (RSCM), and possibly *Lord, for Thy tender mercy's sake* (OUP) which is now attributed to the Elder John Hilton.

ROBERT WHYTE (*c.* 1535–74) was a Roman Catholic musician and the organist of Westminster Abbey (1570–4), who unfortunately died of the plague. He had come to the Abbey from Ely Cathedral, being a kind-hearted person, which is evident in his will that bequeathed 'to every of my scholars to each of them iiij^{d}' (i.e. 'fourpence'). And he was buried in St. Margaret's Church, 'near unto my children.' Morley had a great regard for Whyte's music that included the Compline Motet, *Christe, qui lux es* (OUP), and the Motet for the Office of the Dead *Libera me, Domini* (N).

On July 6th, 1553, the Boy-King Edward VI died from consumption and was succeeded by Mary Tudor, who ploughed on heedless of popular opinion by putting back the clock of reform to the early days of Henrician Catholicism. Many of the monastic houses were restored. And St. Andrew's Day, 1554, saw the Church of England in full communion with the Holy See and the Sarum Rite revived. Worst of all were the heresy burnings that included Thomas Cranmer, who had been Primate of All England for some twenty years—thus creating him into our Martyr-Saint. Four bishops and five deans managed to escape with many Calvinists from Glastonbury to the Continent, but our church musicians continued in their posts and carried on the great tradition of English polyphony.

III. *The Golden Age and the Rise of Puritanism*

Queen Elizabeth was at heart a conservative Catholic and would have desired a more colourful ceremonial in public worship. In her Royal Chapel she insisted in having the ministers dressed in vestments and the Gentlemen of the choir in copes, as well as having the altar set against the east wall with a crucifix and two lights. Nevertheless, she herself had to steer a middle course between the beliefs and practices of the English Catholics and those of the extreme Protestants. At her sister's funeral service the preacher had forewarned her that wolves were coming from Geneva and Germany, having already sent before them their books full of pestilent doctrines that would infect her people.

Discipline was necessary. And the Second Act of Uniformity confirmed the use of The Book of Common Prayer, 'so authorized by Parliament in the said fifth and sixth year of the reign of Edward the Sixth.' Besides the additional Lessons for Sundays and the combination of both the First and Second Edwardine Prayer Books' Words of Administration, the Ornaments Rubric authorized the use of vesture as was worn in the second year of Edward VI's reign. The surplice was used in parish churches, but the cope in cathedrals and collegiate churches.

The new Queen was a supporter of the Arts and was very interested in the raising of musical standards in her choral establishments (Chapel Royal, St. Paul's, St. George's, Windsor, and Westminster Abbey), which she maintained out of her private purse. And she commanded in 1559:

> Because in divers collegiate and also some parish churches there have been livings appointed for the

maintenance of men and children, to use singing in the church, by means whereof the laudable science of music has been had in estimation, no alteration be made of such assignments of living, as heretofore have been appointed to the use of singing or music in the Church, but that the same so remain.

The Rise of Metrical Psalmody

The year 1588 saw the rise of congregational psalmody in England. Strype recorded that before Morning Prayer a Psalm was sung after the Genevan fashion, 'all the congregation— men, women and boys, singing together.' And Bishop Jewell observed that there were six thousand people singing sometimes at St. Paul's Cross in 1560. The legality of metrical psalm-singing had been upheld by the Royal Injunction of 1559, which permitted at the beginning, or at the end, of Morning and Evening Prayer, 'there may be sung *an hymn* or such like song to the praise of Almighty God in the best sort of melody and music that may be conveniently devised.'

The main treasury of congregational praise was *The Whole Booke of Psalmes* (1562), published by John Day and often called The Old Version—hence many of its tunes were nick-named 'Old' (e.g. *Old 100th, Old 124th, Old 125th, Old 81st*). The roots of this Psalter were derived from *The Anglo-Genevan Psalter* (1556) and *The Psalms of David in English Metre* (1558) that were published by the English exiles. The custom of giving some theoretical information to enable the singers to follow the music by a system of *sol-fa* first found its place in this edition, to which was appended *An instruction to learn to sing*.

A year after its first publication, John Day printed a harmonized edition, but with the music written in four part-books. This edition contained several Alternative Versions and an optional instrumental accompaniment for domestic use. Thus, *The Whole Booke of Psalmes* became the official Psalter of English Protestantism; its only rival was *The New Version* (1696), compiled by Nahum Tate and Nicholas Brady.

Another publisher, Thomas Este, printed a metrical Psalm Book (1592), which gave for the first time the tunes with their place-names attached, thus creating another custom in English hymnody. In parish churches, however, the metrical psalms were sung in unison in accordance with Calvinistic practice which aimed at congregational participation in worship; but they were not allowed to replace the Proper Psalms read alternately between the minister and the parish clerk.

The Vestarian Controversy

This was related to Church music indirectly. The whole question of ecclesiastical vesture had already arisen when Bishop Hooper of Gloucester refused to wear the surplice and the rochet as prescribed by the rubrics of the First Edwardine Prayer Book (1549). The Ornaments Rubric, which was inserted into the Prayer Book (1559), restored the use of the Mass vestments, resulting in considerable opposition from the Puritans, as the Queen herself had insisted upon the wearing of the liturgical vestments in her Chapel. And the bishops had to authorize the wearing of the cope in the Communion Service and the surplice in the Daily Offices; yet even Archbishop Parker abysmally failed in his attempts at winning over the English exiles and was forced into publishing the *Advertisements* (1566).

Church music is very much an extra ornament and not an added requirement to the performance of the Prayer Book Services. It can be either elaborate or simple. Whereas the Reformers favoured simplicity, the cathedrals and Chapel Royals inclined towards an over-elaboration in their liturgical music. On the one hand, we have the Master of the Temple, Richard Hooker, defending choral music in worship:

> The Prophet David having therefore singular knowledge not in poetry alone but in music also, judged them (the Psalms) to be things most necessary for the house of God, left behind him to that purpose a number of divinely indited poems, and was further the author of adding unto poetry melody in public

prayer, melody both vocal and instrumental, for the raising up of men's hearts, and the sweetening of their affections towards God. In which considerations the Church of Christ doth likewise at this present day retain it as *an ornament to God's service, and an help to our devotion.*

and, on the other hand, we have the Lady Margaret Professor of Divinity at Cambridge, Thomas Cartwright, viciously attacking choral music, as well as the use of the organ and the antiphonal singing of psalms:

They tosse the Psalms in most places like tennis balls. For the singing Psalms by course and side after side, although it be very ancient yet it is not commendable, and so much the more to be suspected, for that the Devil has gone about to get it so great authority. As for organs and curious singing, though they be proper to popish dens, I mean to cathedral churches, yet some others must also have them. The Queen's Chapel and these churches must be patterns and precedents to the people of all superstitions.

Thus psalmody adopted two lines in England and Scotland: the Calvinists insisted upon congregational and unison singing and the use of the Common Tunes; whereas the liberal-minded churchmen delighted in a more eclectic kind of singing and the use of the four-part Proper Tunes, e.g. William Hunnis's *Seven Sobs of a Sorrowfull Soule* (1583), John Cosyn's *Psalter* (1585), Robert Tailour's *Sacred Hymns* (1615), and *The Scottish Psalter* (1635).

Composers of the Golden Age

WILLIAM BYRD (1543–1623) has been called the Father of English Church Music and was probably born in Lincolnshire, receiving his earlier musical instruction under Thomas Tallis at the Chapel Royal. He was appointed the organist at Lincoln Cathedral when only twenty-one years old. And in

1570 Byrd was sworn in as a Gentleman of the Chapel Royal and was immediately appointed joint-organist with Thomas Tallis to Queen Elizabeth.

Byrd's musical positions afforded him a certain vocational immunity, so that he was able to have his final wish of living and dying 'a true and perfect member of God's holy Catholic Church' fulfilled, and he wrote music for both the Latin and Protestant Rites.

He wrote four Services for the Anglican Rite. *The Great Service* (OUP) was composed for a special occasion and has been called 'the finest unaccompanied setting of the Service in the entire repertory of English Church Music' (Edmund Fellowes). Byrd makes full use of the voices by dividing them into groups of singers, with sections for the *Cantoris* and *Decani* choirs. *The Second Service* (OUP) was written for verses, together with an organ accompaniment that is occasionally independent of the solo voices. There are many sequential phrases in the *Gloria Patri* of the Magnificat. *The Third Service* (OUP) is composed for five parts but it has a simplicity of its own. And *The Short Service* (OUP) possessed no Venite, yet the antiphonal pattern of singing is more intensified. There are no sequential phrases as the composer wanted to follow the strict Cranmerian principle of no repetition in the melodic parts.

Psalmes, Sonets and songs of sadnes and pietie (1588) were dedicated to the Lord Chancellor, Sir Christopher Hatton, and had appended a fascinating note why everyone should learn to sing, including the following reasons:

> It is a singular good remedy for a stuttering and stammering in the speech. It is the only way to know where nature has bestowed the benefit of a good voice: which gift is so rare, as there is not one among a thousand that hath it: and in many that excellent gift is lost, because they want an art to express nature.
>
> The better the voice is, the meeter it is to honour and serve God therewith; and the voice of man is chiefly to be employed to that end.

In this Collection appeared sacred and secular works, including Byrd's *Lullaby Song* and many gay madrigals. Although no Puritan, he opened the book with ten settings of the metrical Psalms.

Psalmes, Songs and Sonnets: some solemne, others joyfull, framed to the Life of the Words (1611) included his well-known anthems: *Sing joyfully* (SB), with its vivacious notes set to the passage 'Blow up the trumpet in the new moon' and other references to musical instruments: *Sing we merrily* (SB); and *This day Christ was born* (SB) with its jubilant text, 'The Archangels are glad,' reaching a climax at 'Glory to God on high.' Other well-known carols are *An earthly tree* (1611, SB) and *From Virgin's womb this day did spring* (1589, SB).

Following his earlier Collection, in conjunction with Thomas Tallis, Byrd wrote two more sets of *Cantiones Sacrae* (1589, 1591), which contained the motets: *O Lord, turn Thy wrath* (OUP), *Bow Thine ear* (CMS), *O praise God in His holiness* (SB), and the inspired *Haec Dies* (OUP) with its syncopated middle section and final flowing *Alleluias*. In an age when the separation between the sacred and the secular was not so marked, these devotional songs and madrigals were sung around the dinner-table in the evening candle-light.

The First Book of *Gradualia* (1605) was dedicated to the Earl of Northampton, who had previously earned the gratitude of the Gentlemen of the Chapel Royal by persuading King James to raise their salaries. But this edition vanished; the Protestants obviously held that Byrd's settings publicized subversive beliefs, because their texts upheld the Catholic devotion to our Lady and the Blessed Sacrament, e.g. the *Ave Maria, gratia plena* (SB) and the equally lovely Sequence Hymn for Corpus Christi, *Ave Verum Corpus* (OUP). However, the Second Book of *Gradualia* was printed in 1607.

There is little doubt that Byrd is one of the greatest composers of Church Music. In setting texts to music he conveys magnificently the mystery of the liturgical action to the singers, ever mindful that the composer is the servant of the liturgical text—concerning which he writes:

There is a certain hidden power, as I learnt by experience, in the thoughts underlying the words themselves; so that, as one meditates upon the sacred words and constantly and seriously considers them, the right notes, in some inexplicable manner, suggest themselves quite spontaneously.

Ave Verum Corpus (OUP) is a good example of pictorialism, e.g. the beautiful expressions, *O dulcis, O pie, O Jesu, Fili Mariae, Miserere mei.* Besides composing the Communion Motets, *Cibavit eos* (SB), *Ego sum panis* (CH), *Sacerdotes Domini* (RSCM) and *O sacrum convivium* (RSCM), Byrd wrote three Masses in about the year 1590, wherein he achieved a complete unification of words and music—thus expressing almost to perfection the divine mystery of the Latin Mass through the instrument of human voices.

The Mass for Five Voices (SB) was the most elaborate setting, though it keeps, as far as possible, to the Cranmerian principle of one note to a syllable. The *Kyrie* is significant for its pathos effected through the frequent use of the minor key, which is the composer's method of picturing man's sorrow for sin. The *Credo* abounds in pictorialism, e.g. the melody of the treble phrase, *Qui sedes,* which is balanced on two notes like children on a seesaw, and the symbols of descent are featured by a leap of a fourth at *ter-rae* and in the alto and bass voices at *descendit.* A wonderful climax occurs in the phrases, *Et resurrexit tertia die* and *Et ascendit in coelum,* where the Ascension is portrayed by the treble and bass voices scaling an octave. Again, human sorrow for sin is perfectly expressed in the *Qui tolis* and *Miserere nobis* of the *Agnus Dei.*

Both Byrd and William Mundy pioneered something original in English Church Music, the use of the solo voice in the anthem. Up to this time, the English Anthem had been modelled upon the structure of the Latin Motet consisting of four or five voices singing in polyphony; but, by introducing the solo voice accompanied by the organ or a consort of viols, they created a more advanced form of the Anthem—

later culminating in the Verse-Anthem of the Restoration period. An excellent example of this type of work is Byrd's Festal Psalm for Epiphany Sunday, *Teach me, O Lord* (CMS), which begins with an instrumental Interlude and then has alternating sections for treble solo and full choir.

Byrd seldom used plainsong melodies. An exception is the chordal setting of the Compline Hymn, *Christe qui lux es et dies* (OUP), wherein the melody of the Second Mode is handed out to a different part in each verse. It is also surprising that Byrd never wrote one single Latin Magnificat or any liturgical music for the organ.

THOMAS MORLEY (1557–1603). A pupil of William Byrd, he was appointed Organist and Master of the Choristers at Norwich at the early age of seventeen, where he remained until 1587. In the following year he sadly lost his infant son, Thomas, and moved with his family to London where he was appointed organist at St. Paul's. He published *A Plaine and Easie Introduction to Practicall Musicke* (1597) which was the first comprehensive guide to the theory of music to be written and published in England. Of particular interest to the student of English Church Music is Morley's theory of 'pictorialism,' the belief that the Arts make their best impression by imitating Nature:

> You must have a care when your matter signifieth 'ascending,' 'high,' 'heaven,' and suchlike you must make your music ascend; and by the contrary where your ditty speaketh of 'descending,' 'lowness,' 'depth,' 'hell,' and others such you must make your music descend; for as it will be thought a great absurdity to talk of heaven and point downwards to the earth, so will it be counted great incongruity if a musician upon the words 'he ascended into heaven' should cause his music descend, or by the contrary upon the descension should cause his music to ascend.[1]

[1] From *A Plain and Easy Introduction to Practical Music*, edited by R. Alec Harman (Dent, 1963), page 291.

52

He kept to the Cranmerian principle—'for every syllable one note'—in setting music to liturgical texts:

> We must also have a care so to apply the notes to the words as in singing there be no barbarism committed; that is that we cause no syllable which is by nature short be expressed by many notes or one long note, nor no long syllables be expressed with a short note.[1]

Morley's church music forms a bridge between the Tudor period and the Restoration. He wrote four Services: the elaborate *First Service 'for verses'* (Morning, Communion and Evening, OUP), the five-part *Second Service*—'Mr. Morley's *Three Minnoms'* (compare with Byrd's five-part Evening Service, SB), the *Short Service* (Evening, OUP), and the earliest surviving setting of the *Burial Service* from The Book of Common Prayer. Many of his anthems have macaronic texts, that is to say, with alternating English and Latin words—e.g. *Nolo mortem peccatoris* (SB).

The Jacobean Age

Many puritans were nursing hopes that the accession of King James I in 1603 would be more favourable towards their cause. In April the King was faced with The Millenary Petition signed by many ministers of the Puritan persuasion, who wished for the Church of England to be released from 'the common burden of human rites and ceremonies,' such as the use of the Cross in Holy Baptism, the Sacrament of Confirmation, the wearing of the surplice, the ring in Holy Matrimony, and especially the lengthy choral services.

At the Hampton Court Conference held in 1604, King James acted as the Chairman. But he failed completely in his relationships with the Puritans, who had now grown into an influential movement in England. The Conference, however, did decide to embark upon a new translation of the Bible that materialized in the publication of The Authorized Version of 1611. And the Puritan hopes of replacing The Elizabethan Prayer Book (1559) with John Knox's Genevan

Service Book (1556) were shattered by the authorization of The Jacobean Prayer Book (1604). This Prayer Book was a minor revision of The Elizabethan Book, but with the addition of the Second Part of the Catechism containing some Questions-and-Answers on the Sacraments, which had been abbreviated from the Middle and Little Catechisms of Dean Alexander Nowell (1560–1602), in response to the Puritan request for a fuller statement of the Faith.

Moreover, whereas the Reformed churches in Europe and the Separatist meeting-houses in England were both cold and unfriendly in atmosphere, the same could not be held against the Jacobean churches. They were abounding in warmth, with their beautifully-carved screens, pulpits and pews. It is not in any way surprising to discover that the church music of this period was equally colourful and richly ornamented.

Composers of the Age

THOMAS TOMKINS (1572–1656), born at St. David's in Pembrokeshire, came from 'a family that produced more capable musicians, during the sixteenth and seventeenth centuries, than any other which England can boast' (Burney). He succeeded Nathaniel Patrick as organist at Worcester Cathedral in 1596, where he remained until 1646 when his appointment was terminated by the circumstances of the Commonwealth. It is certain that Tomkins regarded the composition of church music as an essential part of his activity as a cathedral organist. But its publication was another matter; and he left it to his son, Nathaniel, to collect his sacred music into ten books that were published in 1688.

Furthermore, one of these books of the *Musica Deo Sacra et Ecclesiae Anglicanae* contained a full organ-part, having the distinction of being the only printed organ book in seventeenth century England:

> In the verse anthems, or 'Songs to the Organ,' Tomkins has left a solid and impressive monument to the taste of the times, a taste which he, as a virtuoso organist,

54

showed to a large degree. Only in the verse anthem was it possible for the instrument to become a vital, creative part of the texture: it stood on a par with the voices, supporting them in the choruses as well as it did in the full anthems, but besides this it gave life and meaning to the solos and smaller ensembles, that are so important a feature of the Jacobean verse anthem.[2]

In this great collection, there are many anthems for special occasions—Coronations, Festal Days, Communion and Burial Services. Tomkins liked to set to music the texts from the Prayer Book Collects, e.g. *Almighty and everlasting God* (H) for Ash Wednesday, and *God, who as at this time* (H) for Whitsunday. There is a metrical version of Psalm 23, *My shepherd is the living Lord* (SB), where there are used too many sequential phrases, e.g. 'For His most holy name, for His most holy name, for His most holy, most holy, holy name, for His most holy name'! Of his seven Services, the most popular is the *First Evening Service* (N); and the *Third Service* (OUP), called The Great Service, and the *Fifth Service* (OUP) are for verses. Tomkins has written, too, Festal Psalms, settings of the First and Second Litanies, and Responses (CMS).

THOMAS WEELKES (*c.* 1575–1623) was appointed the organist at Winchester College in 1598, for which he received a salary of thirteen shillings and fourpence with free board and lodging. He was also the organist of Chichester Cathedral from 1602 until his death. Of his ten Services, only the *Short Service* (SB) and three settings of the Evening Canticles (OUP) have survived. As a composer Weelkes delighted in dramatic pictorialism and bold harmonizations, e.g. the ascending treble passages—'All in glory's highest key' and 'Unto praise's highest part'—in the well-known anthem, *Gloria in excelsis Deo* (OUP); and the simultaneous rests in *Hosanna to the Son of David* (OUP) that allow his rich harmonies to echo around the church building.

[2] From *Thomas Tomkins* by Denis Stevens (Macmillan, 1957), page 88.

ORLANDO GIBBONS (1583–1625), the youngest son of a very musical family, was baptized in Oxford on Christmas Day 1583. He studied music under his eldest brother, Edward Gibbons, who was then the organist at King's College, Cambridge. At the early age of twenty-one, Orlando Gibbons was appointed one of the organists at the Chapel Royal. Both King James and the Queen befriended him and rewarded him for faithful service by considerable financial assistance. The King himself appointed Gibbons as one of the Musicians for the Virginals; and in 1623 he was made the organist at Westminster Abbey. But two years later, when senior organist of the Chapel Royal, Gibbons travelled to Canterbury where the Court were to meet the new Queen. He never did meet her, for he died from an apoplectic fit and was buried in the Cathedral on Whitsunday.

Orlando Gibbons, a loyal Anglican, never set one single Latin text to music. His magnificent services and anthems were written to serve the religious needs of *The Book of Common Prayer* and an age that read *The Authorized Version* of the Scriptures. He wrote two Services: *The Short Service* (OUP) and *The Verse Service in D Minor* (OUP). The former alternates between homophonic and polyphonic styles of harmony, yet affording places for *Decani* and *Cantoris* singing as well as sections for full choir. And the latter work is more elaborate with verses for different groups of soloists and with places for organ interludes. The *Te Deum* has a fine contrapuntal passage, 'Thou art the King of Glory, O Christ,' and a sad sequential phrase, 'the sharpness of death.'

He wrote about forty anthems, of which a third were written in the polyphonic idiom, e.g. *O clap your hands* (OUP), and the remainder looked forward to the verse-anthem of the Restoration period, by containing sections for solo voices and independent organ accompaniments. On special occasions the organ was replaced by a consort of viols and possibly by two bands, each consisting of six or seven cornets and sackbuts, especially at the Chapel Royal where the musical resources were greater than elsewhere.

Orlando Gibbons loved to dramatize scenes from the Bible.

See, the Word is incarnate (SB) is a colourful but carefully-planned verse-anthem, with pictorial phrases—'The law is cancelled . . . Jews and Gentiles all converted . . . diseases cured . . . the dead are raised . . . the earth quakes, the sun is darkened, the powers of hell are shaken . . . the serpent's head is bruised, Christ's kingdom exalted.' Considerable movement is achieved throughout *Hosanna to the Son of David* (OUP) by using alternating groups of solo verses with sections for full choir. This work in many ways sounds like a peal of church bells. Another dramatic anthem is *Glorious and powerful God* (N) that opens with an outstanding bass solo, similar to some of Purcell's compositions.

This is the record of John (OUP) dedicated to the President of St. John's College, Oxford, Dr. Laud, who later became Archbishop of Canterbury, is accompanied by viols; and the composer handles the text with great sensitivity—particularly at the musical phrases: 'From Jerusalem' (bars 7–9), 'Art thou Elias?' (bars 26–8), and 'Make straight the way of the Lord' (bars 56–62). The full choir sections are introduced homophonically and afterwards are developed into miniature fugues. A similar verse-anthem is *Almighty God, who by the Son* (OUP), with its text based upon the Collect for St. Peter's Day.

Gibbons wrote seventeen hymn-tunes that were published, all except one, in George Wither's *Hymns and Songs of the Church* (1623). But only the treble and the bass lines were supplied. These tunes had unusual metres because they were composed for words where no existing psalm-tune would fit; hence the curious numbering corresponded to the serial-numbering in Wither's book. The following tunes have appeared in *Hymns Ancient and Modern Revised,* unless otherwise stated: *Song 1* (402), *Song 4* (EH 113), *Song 5* (164), *Song 9* (Oxford Hymn Book, 233), *Song 13* (105), *Song 18* (EH 357), *Song 20* (EH 442), *Song 22* (238), *Song 24* (397), *Song 34* (336), *Song 47* or *46* (358) and *Song 67* (571).

Concern for the beauty of holiness was a common desire of both the Laudians and the Puritans. Whereas the former saw this ideal in external forms of ceremonial and liturgical music, the latter regarded this ideal as a matter for the inner spirit of man's soul. If the Laudians upheld the dignity of worship by means of beautiful buildings, stained-glass windows and ornate organ-cases, the Puritans proclaimed the moral code of God by means of the preaching of the Word, the practice of Bible-reading and the singing of metrical psalms. And in 1643 the Long Parliament appointed a Synod, called the Westminster Assembly, to discuss possible reforms of the Anglican liturgy and of the constitution of the Established Church. Therefore in place of The Book of Common Prayer they issued *The Directory of Public Worship* (1645), which formed a set of religious instructions rather than a collection of revised services. Sunday worship consisted of prayers, two Bible-readings, metrical psalm-singing and a sermon. Afterwards came the celebration of the Lord's Supper, but with the congregations sitting this time around the communion-table in the main body of the church and with their ministers facing them. In the words of the late Dr. Henry Phillips:

> The purifying of public worship was complete. A model was given for all future nonconformist services. The puritan mind, indeed, started its reasoning from the axiom that in public worship all expression is immoral, the inner feeling needing no material manifestation. Carried to its logical end it becomes Quakerism; but most of the Puritans of the Rebellion would not go so far. They allowed kneeling, they allowed psalm-tunes, though they shuddered at surplices and choir-music.[3]

This explains William Child's retirement to a farm in order to write church music, which included the anthem, *O Lord God, the heathen are come into Thine inheritance* (BP), 'com-

[3] From *The Singing Church* (Faber & Faber, 1945), page 107.

posed in the year 1644 on the occasion of the abolishing The Common Prayer Book and the overthrowing the Constitution both in Church and State.'

Nevertheless, a considerable flexibility in the conduct of public worship was experienced during these troubled times. The diaryist, John Evelyn, recorded that there was at least one London church using the Prayer Book Services. And Bishop Warner of Rochester was accustomed to reading the Daily Offices and administering the Sacraments when required. Cromwell himself even permitted the senior officers to conduct prayers and sometimes to preach.

This lack of uniformity resulted in the birth of Independent worship. At Exeter Cathedral, for example, a partition separated the Presbyterian worshippers from the Independents. Toleration had clearly come to be accepted in public worship. In fact, up to the year 1644 the choir at King's College, Cambridge, was maintained at full strength. The next year saw a gradual decline in its numbers. And in 1653 the choir consisted of six lay-clerks and eleven boys. Although there were no choirboys left after 1654, the organist, Henry Loosemore, still drew his stipend and the allowance for teaching them.

The main reason why the Puritans objected to instrumental music in worship was scriptural. The employment of instruments in public worship was in accordance with the worship of the Temple and of the Old Covenant, whereas the Puritan ideal of a more spiritual worship was held to be in keeping with the new teaching of the New Covenant as expounded by Christ. Therefore in 1644 the Commons authorized 'the speedy demolishing of all organs—the better to accomplish the blessed Reformation so happily begun, and to remove all offences and things illegal in the worship of God.' This attitude was nothing new in the history of the English Church because the Lower House of the Convocation of Canterbury had already endeavoured to pass a resolution for their removal in 1562; and its sponsors were none other than the deans of St. Paul's, Hereford and Exeter!

It must be recalled that organ-playing had become too

elaborate with unnecessary florid runs, which made congregational participation in the singing extremely difficult. One wonders whether the English organists wept as the organist at Zurich did when he watched the heavy axes falling upon his beloved instrument? Or whether the Worcestershire people lamented after observing their cathedral's organ-case being made into a bedstead for some lazy ecclesiastic? However, we know that some organs were sold to private individuals, who used them for chamber music—among whom was Oliver Cromwell who had the organ in Magdalen College Chapel, Oxford, placed in the gallery of Hampton Court Palace. Other instruments were transferred to taverns, or 'music houses,' where they were used for secular interludes in-between the beer-drinking.

The often-quoted statement of Charles Burney, that during the Commonwealth 'ten years of gloomy silence seem to have elapsed before a string was suffered to vibrate, or a pipe to breathe aloud, in the kingdom,' is completely groundless. Although the Puritans objected to all forms of elaborate singing and instrumental music in worship, they did allow music and dancing to be performed in the domestic setting. And it is interesting to record that the Royalist John Wilson, who was Professor of Music at Oxford, was permitted to publish his *Psalterium Carolinum: The devotions of his sacred Majesty in his solitudes and sufferings, rendered into verse set for three voices, and an organ or theorbo* (1652); and that the parish clerk of the Temple Church, John Playford, who was also an important music publisher, was allowed to own a music shop in the Inner Temple near the church door, where he sold copies of his *Dancing Master* (1651) and his wife advertised her dancing school! Furthermore, another strong Royalist, Sir William D'Avenant, was granted permission to build the first English opera house in 1656.

Psalm-singing increased in popularity among both the Royalists and the Puritans. The Roundhead troops sang many of the metrical psalms while they were marching through the country-side. Because the ordinary people were either unable to afford their own copies of the psalters, or were illiterate, there arose the custom of *lining-out* the psalms, which was officially authorized in 1644:

> That the whole congregation may join herein, every one that can read is to have a psalm-book, and all others, not disabled by age or otherwise, are to be exhorted to learn to read. But for the present, where many in the congregation cannot read, it is convenient that the minister, or some fit person appointed by him and the other ruling officers, do read the psalm line by line before the singing thereof.

It was a former chorister of St. Paul's Cathedral, Thomas Ravenscroft, who published *The Whole Book of Psalms: with the Hymns Evangelical and Songs Spiritual, composed in four parts* (1621). And Henry Lawes provided twenty-four tunes for George Sandys' *A Paraphrase upon the Divine Poems* (1638), of which Lawes' tunes *Battle, Falkland, Farley Castle, Psalm 32* and *Whitehall* have reappeared in modern hymn books. These tunes are distinctive for their high finishes, operatic style and for their unusual turns of phrase similar to the opening bars of the well-known tune, *St. Anne.* And with his brother William, Lawes also published *Choice Psalms* (1648) that were dedicated to Charles I, who was martyred within a few months of their publication. William Child also wrote the *First Set of Psalms for three voices fit for private chapels, or rather private meetings with the continual bass, either for the organ or theorbo, newly composed after the Italian way* (1639).

Finally, Oliver Cromwell himself did much to encourage music in England. He instructed Cambridge University to admit Benjamin Rogers to the degree of Bachelor of Music in 1658. And he asked his private organist, John Hingston, to train two choirboys so that they might sing Richard Deering's Latin motets.

IV. *The Restoration and the Splendour of the Chapel Royal*

The Restoration of the Monarchy revivified English church music. And yet it cannot be held that King Charles II was completely responsible for the secularization of the verse-anthem, because other composers had already written and performed this type of work with an instrumental accompaniment. What the Restoration composer did was to write Church music in the *genre* of his times, which was just as much influenced by the past as by the present.

The same age saw a renewed interest in liturgical matters. The choral eucharist was re-introduced at Durham and Exeter. And when the Convocations met to discuss a possible revision of the *Elizabethan Prayer Book* no drastic changes were made: the *Black Rubric* was restored, but with the words 'reall and essencial presence' amended to 'Corporeal Presence.' And a new intercession for the departed was inserted at the end of the Prayer for the Church:

> And we also bless thy holy name for all thy servants departed this life in thy faith and fear; beseeching thee to give us grace so to follow their good examples, that with them we may be partakers of thy heavenly kingdom.

But a retrograde step was seen in the directive extending the use of Ante-Communion to include not only Holy Days but Sundays, thus leaving the celebration of Holy Communion to three or four times a year. Moreover, the State Prayers were transferred from the Litany in the Book of 1637 to the end of the Daily Offices. And most important of all for English Church Music was the insertion of the rubric: *In Quires and Places where they sing, here followeth the Anthem.*

There were drastic changes both in the musical style and the performance of choral services in the Chapel Royal, since for sixteen years no music had been sung in our choral establishments apart from the metrical psalms of Sternhold and Hopkins. To supplement the chorister's singing, small treble wind instruments were employed in places like Westminster Abbey even up to 1664. These cornets, as they were called, were made from wood and had cup-shaped mouthpieces and finger holes.

At the time of the Coronation in 1661, the staff of the Chapel Royal consisted of nine Ministers and nineteen Gentlemen, including Thomas Purcell and his famous son, Henry. Then there were the Master of the Children (Captain Cooke), the three organists (William Child, Christopher Gibbons and Edward Lowe), the Clerk of the Cheque (Henry Lawes), the Sergeant of the Vestry, the two Yeomen and the Groom.

No wonder people flocked to Whitehall in order to hear the latest style in English Church Music, as well as to listen to the Royal Band of twenty-four string-players in imitation of Louis XIV's one at Versailles. Whereas some patrons were impressed like the Diarist, Samuel Pepys: 'To Whitehall Chapel, where sermon almost done, and I heard Captain Cooke's new Music. This is the first day of having vials and other instruments to play a symphony between every verse of the anthems; but the music more full than it was the last Sunday, and very fine it is' (September 14th, 1662), others had less favourable comments to make over the introduction of secular instruments into the sacred surroundings of public worship. Another famous Diarist, John Evelyn, remarks: 'Instead of the ancient, grave and solemn wind music accompanying the organ was introduced a concert of twenty-four violins every pause (in the anthem) after the French fantastical light way, better suiting a tavern or playhouse than a church. This was the first time of change, and now we no more heard the cornet which gave life to the organ' (December 21st,

1662). Yet Evelyn was mistaken in saying that it was the first time of change, since we have Pepys' evidence of an earlier date. And in the second volume of his *Collection of Cathedral Music* (1716) Dr. Tudway observes:

> His Majesty who was a brisk and airy prince, coming to the Crown in the flower and vigour of his age, was soon, if I may say so, tired with the grave and solemn way, and ordered the composers of his Chapel to add symphonies, etc. with instruments to their anthems; and thereupon established a select number of his private music to play the symphonies and ritornellos which he had appointed. The old Masters of Music, Dr. Child, Mr. Gibbons, Mr. Lowe, etc., organists to His Majesty, hardly knew how to comport themselves with these new-fangled ways, but proceeded in their compositions according to the old style, and therefore there are only some services and full anthems of theirs to be found.

The appointment of Captain Cooke (1616–72) whose father was a Gentleman of the Chapel Royal and who had been himself a Child of the Chapel, was a foresighted step towards the reform of this choral establishment. Cooke possessed not only an excellent bass voice, having studied singing in Italy, but also a sense of military discipline which he had acquired during his Captaincy in the Royalist Army.

The Restoration age was one of the individual performer. With excellent solo voices like the Reverend John Gostling's, who possessed the range of a Russian bass, and the alto voices of William Child and Michael Wise, the verse anthem came to the forefront of English church music. And it is somewhat curious to find that fine boys' voices of the Chapel Royal were never used in the solo movements; perhaps social convention demanded that only grown-ups were to sing solos—Gentlemen who wanted above everything else to win social prestige at Court: 'I could discern Captain Cooke,' writes Samuel Pepys, 'to overdo his part at singing which I never did before.'

Composers delighted in the use of modulation and the figured bass; the last is ably demonstrated in Purcell's *Evening Hymn* (OUP) with its glorious Hallelujahs at the end. As the main emphasis was upon solo-singing, so both chorus and orchestra took a minor part by way of contrast. Thus it was left to the eighteenth century composers like Handel to develop choral singing. Whereas the Chapel Royal choir was composed of highly-skilled singers, the cathedral choirs were very much dependent upon the help of part-time singers.

A marked feature of the verse anthem was the use of numerous instrumental interludes, called *ritornelli* or symphonies. And it was the custom in the verse anthem for the strings to play the symphonies and the organ to accompany the solo movements. However, instrumental interludes were not allowed in the performance of the Canticles. There were very few settings of the Communion Service at this time. The Shorter Services eventually led to the simple Anglican Chant and psalm-tune, both very popular with the Puritans who upheld the necessity for congregational participation in public worship. This period of church music saw, too, the introduction of the bar-line into anthems and services.

The Importance of the Psalter in Worship

This can be seen in two ways. Firstly, it was employed in parish churches for metrical psalm-singing. In 1671 John Playford published *Psalms & Hymns in Solemn Musick of Foure Parts on the Common Tunes to the Psalms in Metre: used in Parish Churches*. The melody of these metrical psalms was placed in the tenor line, and the settings were composed for two counter-tenors and one bass voice. However, when treble voices were available they assisted in the singing of the tenor part. This Collection proved to be too highbrow for the needs of the village congregation; besides, the hymns were derived mostly from John Austin's *Devotions in the Antient Way of Offices* (Paris, 1668), which was a Roman Catholic manual. Thus Playford was forced into lowering his previous standards by issuing *The Whole Book of Psalms*

65

(1667) which immediately became the recognized psalm-book for the remainder of the century and for the greater part of the eighteenth century. This time the tunes were set in three parts but with the melody placed in the upper parts, because in most parish churches there would be only two parts—the melody and the bass. And in his *Preface* Playford gives some sound advice, namely:

> It would be much to the advancement of this Divine Service of singing Psalms if the Clergy would more generally addict themselves to the study of Music, and give themselves some little trouble in assisting their several congregations with their skill. And also if they would make a choice of such persons for their Clerks, as have either some skill in song, or at least a tunable voice and good ear to learn. And here I cannot but commend the Parish Clerks in London, who for the improvement of Music have set up an organ in their Common-Hall where they meet once a fortnight, and have an organist to attend them to practise the singing of Psalms: which custom (if not neglected) will much augment their skill, to their reputation and the better performing the Service of the Church.

Secondly, the Psalter formed a popular treasury of texts for composers, affording them even more scope for choruses, solos and quartets. A difference is to be seen between the length of texts chosen by the sixteenth-century composers and of those selected by the Restoration ones, who preferred the longer settings of complete psalms, e.g. Purcell's *O sing unto the Lord* (Psalm 96), comprising three hundred and twenty-seven bars of music.

Directions on the Choral Service for Precentors

During the Restoration and after, a few instruction books on the conduct of worship in cathedrals and elsewhere were published to help priests, who had forgotten the essential rudiments because of the rebellion and the prohibition of

The Book of Common Prayer in 1644. The organist of Christ Church Cathedral, Oxford, Edward Lowe, published *A Short Direction for the Performance of Cathedral Service* (1661), in which information was included as to how the Preces and Responses and Litany were sung during the Tudor period of English church music, together with a version of Thomas Tallis's *Extraordinary Responses upon Festivalls*. Further, the second edition of 1664 bore the grand title: *A Review of some short Directions formerly printed, for the Performance of Cathedral Service, with many useful Additions according to the Common Prayer-book, as it is now established. Published for the Information of such as are ignorant in the Performance of that Service, and shall be called to officiate in cathedral or collegiate Churches; or any other that religiously desire to bear a Part in that Service.*

Another instruction book was published by a Minor Canon of St. Paul's Cathedral, James Clifford, entitled: *Collection of the Divine Services and Anthems usually sung in his Majesties Chapel, and in all the Cathedrals and Collegiate Choirs of the Church of England and Ireland* (1663). A second edition was published a year later, which included chants for all the Prayer Book Canticles and their alternatives.

The Auditory Church

An outcome of the Fire of London, which saw the destruction of eighty-four city churches, was the auditory or room-church. An Act of Parliament in 1708 provided for the building of fifty new churches in the London area. And the architect of St. Paul's Cathedral, Sir Christopher Wren (1632–1723), was appointed by the Crown to supervise this mammoth undertaking. Wren outlined in a personal letter to one of his friends the basic requirements for these new buildings. He held that no church building should be built to seat more than 2,000 people, so that they could all 'hear distinctly and see the preacher.' And in the placing of the pulpit he observed that a moderate voice could be audible fifty feet in front of the preacher and thirty feet on either side of him. Moreover, he affirmed that a Frenchman would be heard better than an Englishman because he was taught to raise his voice at the end of sentences. He also stipulated that churches should be sixty feet broad and ninety feet long, and that the buildings should not be fitted with pews since benches were better.

Hence the auditory church was divided into three liturgical units: the font placed next to the west door, the pews positioned in easy sight of both the pulpit and reading-desk, and the altar only seen when the communicants walked forward to kneel down at the east end—since the three-decker pulpit was placed in the middle of the aisle. Whenever there was an assistant-priest the vicar would preside from the pulpit, the curate from the reading-desk, and the parish clerk from his pew.

The Composers of the Age

PELHAM HUMPHREY (1647–74) was appointed the Head Child at the Chapel Royal in 1660. At seventeen years old he had not only composed five anthems but was sent abroad with a grant of £200 from the Secret Service Fund, which enabled Humphrey to further his musical studies under the Director of Music at Versailles, Jean Baptiste Lully, who taught him the art of the free-rhythmical recitative; and Humphrey was called 'a singer after the Italian manner.'

He returned to England in 1667 and immediately took up his former appointment as a Gentleman of the Chapel Royal. And Samuel Pepys informs that little Pelham Humphrey 'is an absolute Monsieur, as full of form, and confidence, and vanity, and disparages everything and everybody's skill but his own.' He also married the daughter of Captain Cooke and was appointed, upon his father-in-law's death in 1672, the Master of the Children and Composer to the Chapel Royal.

His *Evening Service in E minor* (N) followed the Tudor custom of dividing words into their vowel-sounds, e.g. 'sal-vat-ion' and 'gen-er-at-ion,' etc. He also wrote a popular chant to Psalm 150 (*The Grand Chant*).[1]

[1] *Parish Psalter:* Chant 242.

Many of his anthems contain symphonies for strings, with the organ continuo left to the ingenuity of the organist, who would no doubt embroider it with shakes and other musical ornaments as there were no pedals in those days. *O Lord my God* (BP) is an extended verse anthem, whose variety of texture is derived from its miniature symphonies and sections for declamatory solos and for full choir. Pictorialism is evident in the musical phrases, 'All my bones are out of joint. . . . My heart is even like melting wax' (bars 56–74), 'The council of the wicked layeth siege against me,' and 'They pierced my hands and my feet' (bars 113–29). The late Professor Walker's criticism that Humphrey's music portrays 'a highly talented but superficial youth, with whom desire for immediate popularity among the admirers of the new style was the strongest motive' seems too harsh an assessment of a musician who died at the early age of twenty-seven. His anthems include *Hear, O heavens* (OUP) and *Hymn to God the Father* (SCH).

MICHAEL WISE (1648–87) was appointed the organist at Salisbury Cathedral in 1668, and a Gentleman of the Chapel Royal. His untimely death was caused by a quarrel with his wife, which ended with his escaping into one of the Salisbury streets, after curfew, and knocking down the night-watchman who recovered first and killed Wise with his bill-hook.

He has written at least three dozen anthems, of which *Awake up my Glory* (N) and *Prepare ye the way* (N) are excellent examples of the Restoration verse-anthem, with its miniature sections for instrumental interludes, solos and full choir, which required to be extended into a full work. *The ways of Zion do mourn* (AHC) is a verse-anthem for Holy Week; it is marked by a charming simplicity, with the narrative given to the bass soloist and with the treble soloist's added comments: 'For these things I weep,' etc. He also wrote a Service in D minor (OUP), a Short Service in E Flat (OUP) and the anthems: *Awake, awake, put on thy strength* (N) and *Thy beauty, O Israel* (N).

JOHN BLOW (1649–1708) was appointed Gentleman of the Chapel Royal and Master of the Children (1674). He was the first musician to have conferred upon him the Lambeth degree of Doctor of Music through the favour of Archbishop Sancroft, in 1677. Apart from the years when his pupil, Henry Purcell, held the position,[2] Blow was the organist of Westminster Abbey from 1668 until his death.

Blow ranks, indeed, as one of the most accomplished of English Church musicians, only to be surpassed by his famous pupil, Henry Purcell. He wrote both sacred and secular works. His Church music comprises eight Complete Services, eleven Latin Motets which were composed for the Queen's Roman Catholic Chapel at Somerset House, and many anthems, of which some were written for special occasions: *Behold, O God our defender* (SB), *God spake sometimes in visions* (SB), and *Let thy hand be strengthened* (SB) for James II's Coronation in 1685; *O Lord, I have sinned* (N) for General Monck's funeral in 1670; and *Praise the Lord, O my soul* (OUP) for the Thanksgiving Service in celebration of the Peace of Ryswick in 1697.

The Restoration composer wrote much music expressing man's grief and utter desolation, since the fact of sudden death was always preoccupying his mind. Of his Latin Motets, Blow's *Salvator Mundi* (BP) is a good example of this experience, wherein pathetic beauty is symbolized in the music's chromaticism and in the restrained pictorialism of words translated into music; the text itself was taken from the Antiphon used at Holy Unction. And Blow himself expressed the wish that the Motet should be sung at the Prayer Book Occasional Office for the Visitation of the Sick.

HENRY PURCELL (1659–95) came from a family of musicians. Both his father and uncle were Gentlemen of the Chapel Royal. However, his father died when he was six years old; and his uncle adopted Henry as his own son. Purcell was admitted as a Child of the Chapel and studied under Captain Cooke for eight years and also under Pelham Humphrey. He

[2] Henry Purcell was organist at Westminster Abbey from 1679 to 1695.

obviously possessed an excellent ear for music, having been appointed organ-tuner at Westminster Abbey when his voice broke at fourteen years old.

He was appointed in 1679 organist of Westminster Abbey at the annual salary of £10, where he remained until his death. There he had the oversight of the four minor canons, twelve lay-clerks and ten choristers—a smaller choir than the Chapel Royal's which then numbered thirty-two Gentlemen, eight minor canons and several Children. In 1682 he was appointed one of the three organists to the Chapel Royal and Master of the Children. In the words of Jeremy Noble:

> Originally there had been no specific post of organist in the Chapel Royal; organists had been drawn from among those Gentlemen with a particular aptitude for keyboard-playing. But during the seventeenth century the organists' special function came to be acknowledged officially and from the Restoration onwards it was normal for three to hold office at any one time.[3]

In the following year Purcell was appointed Keeper of the King's Instruments and then Harpsichordist, or Conductor, of the King's Private Musick in 1685. After this date he wrote little Church music; firstly because his attention was directed towards writing secular music for odes and masques, secondly because King James possessed his own Roman Catholic chapel in Whitehall in 1688 which resulted in a decline of courtly interest in the musical establishment of the Chapel Royal and the discarding of instrumental symphonies from the verse anthems. Thus the style of the English Anthem changed in order to meet the small resources of provincial choirs, who had no string players at their disposal.

Whereas Purcell wrote Full Anthems with an organ accompaniment to double the voice parts, others could be sung without any accompaniment at all, e.g. *Hear my prayer*

[3] From *Henry Purcell, 1659–1695: Essays on his Music* (OUP, 1959), edited by Imogen Holst, page 65.

(1682, N). In these anthems Purcell continued in the great tradition of sixteenth-century polyphony, although assimilating that tradition within his own idiom. Of his seventy anthems, the five-part setting of the Latin Psalm, *Jehova quam multi sunt hostes* (N), is probably his finest achievement in church music. It is written in alternating chordal and contrapuntal harmony; yet there are good examples of dramatic recitative, e.g. the bass solo *Surge, Surge, Jehova*, and the tenor *Gloria mea* with its brilliantly-written triple rhythms. And this work is essentially pictorial in style, which is so beautifully achieved in the short chorus, *Ergo cubui et dormivi*.

And we must not forget the fine anthems expressing the emotional experience of both joy and sadness: the Ascension-tide *O all ye people* (N), the Litany Verse *Remember not, Lord, our offences* (N), and *The Burial Service* (N) which includes the simple setting of the words, *Thou knowest, Lord, the secrets of our hearts* (N), which was originally accompanied by 'flat Mournfull Trumpets' (i.e. slide-trumpets) at Queen Mary's Funeral in 1695.

Next, there were the verse-anthems with organ accompaniment, e.g. *Thy word is a lantern* (N), with its fine alto recitative and its swinging *Hallelujahs* in the final chorus. Under this category comes the pathetic setting of the Passion-tide Prophecies from the Prophet Isaiah, *Who hath believed our report?* (N). Finally, there were the anthems with instrumental symphonies and accompaniments; but with the organ occasionally used by way of contrast in the solo movements, e.g. *I will give thanks* (BP), *My heart is inditing* (SCH), *O sing unto the Lord* (N), and *Rejoice in the Lord*—'The Bell Anthem' (N).

Purcell was a tone-poet who delighted in setting to music scenes from the pages of the Old Testament. His verse anthem, *My beloved spake* (N) is a work of thanksgiving for the awakening of Spring, wherein the composer employs imitation in the opening verse through the three solo voices reiterating the word, 'Rise.' Compare, too, the exquisite harmonies and melodies in the passages: 'The rain is over and gone,' 'The flow'rs appear upon the earth,' and the pictorialism of 'the voice of the turtle.' Then there are the dramatic, if not operatic, scenes in *The Blessed Virgin's Expostulation* (BH), *Job's Curse* (BH), and *Saul and the Witch of Endor* (BH).

Purcell broke away from the Cranmerian principle of 'one note for every syllable' by writing florid passages (*coloratura*), like the fine bass solo's portrayal of ocean billows in *They that go down to the sea in ships* (N). No wonder 'no other vocal Music was listened to with pleasure for nearly thirty years after Purcell's death; when they gave way only to the favourite opera songs of Handel' (Burney).

Purcell himself was a Royalist and a Catholic at heart. And he utilized the Anthem on important occasions to reflect the political situation of his times; hence considerable care was taken in the choice of unliturgical texts from the Bible. For example, the anthem *Who hath believed our report?* (1679–80) was selected with its apposite text to commemorate the martyrdom of King Charles I. Other Restoration Anthems featured Charles II as King David, Monmouth as Absalom, and the Duchess of Portsmouth as Bathsheba! In fact, they represented 'the royal (i.e. Tory) position in musical dress' (Franklin Zimmerman).[4]

His *Te Deum and Jubilate in D* (N) is theatrical in its idiom, with its use of martial trumpets, organ and strings; and was written for the opening of the new St. Paul's Cathedral, designed by Sir Christopher Wren, though the composer sadly never lived to see its completion. Purcell's other settings of the Anglican Services comprise the large *Service in B Flat* (OUP) and the *Evening Canticles in G Minor* (OUP), composed in the verse-anthem style—though the Gloria of the Nunc Dimittis is attributed to Mr. Ralph Roseingrave, who was the organist of Dublin Cathedral.

On November 21st, 1695, Henry Purcell died from tuberculosis upon the Eve of the annual St. Cecilia's Day celebrations; and his life-long association with the Abbey is

[4] Viz. *Henry Purcell, His Life and Times* by F. B. Zimmerman (Macmillan, 1967), pages 166–75.

remembered in modern hymn-books through the tune *West-minster Abbey* (620) that has been adapted from the Halle-lujahs of his anthem, *O God, Thou art my God* (N).[5]

JEREMIAH CLARKE (*c.* 1673–1707) was appointed organist at Winchester, and next at the rebuilt St. Paul's Cathedral in 1695, where he remained organist until his sudden death. Clarke's music abounds in tuneful melodies. He wrote two Services and many anthems, of which *I will love Thee* (N) is characteristic for its duets, e.g. the thunder and lightning movement with its brilliant accompaniment. And his hymn-tunes were usually written in triple-time and possessed a feminine, operatic style about them: compare the delicate *Bishopsthorpe* (AMR 208), *King's Norton* (EH 419), and *Uffingham* (HCS 287) with the more virile tunes: *Hermon* (HCS 170) and *St. Magnus* (AMR 218).

The Restoration witnessed the secularization of the sacred music in the Chapel Royal, after several violins had been introduced there, for it must be recalled that the violin was very much associated with dancing. Moreover, composers like Humphrey, Blow, Purcell and Wise wrote anthems in the rhythms of both the minuet and the saraband. This new religious music was as much English as that of Vaughan Williams is to-day.

---

[5] Christopher Steel has written a *Fantasy on a Theme of Purcell* (N), which is based upon this hymn-tune.

V. *The Age of the Gallery Minstrels and of the Oratorio*

The eighteenth century has come under much criticism from the pen of the historian. The late Norman Sykes admitted that neither liturgical composition nor study were among the eminent gifts of this age. And the individual, such as the saintly Dr. Samuel Johnson, preferred to worship their Maker quietly and to remain undisturbed by the apathy of contemporary worship in the Established Church, which suffered from a lack of adventure and renewal. 'The beauty of the English Church in this time,' wrote Dean Church, 'was its family life of purity and simplicity; its blot was quiet wordliness.' A gradual decay of sacramental life went hand in hand with a rapid decline of weekday services. It needed more than the fellowship of the Gallery Minstrels and the enthusiasm of the Methodists to jolt people from the rut of rationalist philosophy and latitudinarian religion.

Due to the Enlightenment, a considerable secularization had taken place within the Church. The Gothic architecture of the past had now been replaced by more Classical styles in church building, which made our parish churches into Greek temples and spacious ballrooms. Our provincial cathedrals had little to offer musically because of the disgraceful neglect by their chapters. Moreover, when the organist of Durham Cathedral was promoted to Rochester in 1790, Mr. Ralph Banks discovered that the Cathedral had only one lay-clerk on weekdays, two settings of the Canticles were used, and only seven anthems were sung in rotation on Sundays during the previous twelve years.

This was the age of the foreign musician's sojourn in London. The eminent Dr. Maurice Greene bows to the Master Handel, takes off his coat and pumps the organ in

St. Paul's Cathedral for him. And, what is more, the entire musical world was dominated by the *primo donnas* and the *primo nomos,* for whose voices our composers had to write special music.

And just as the Restoration church music was influenced by continental and secular styles, so the eighteenth century incorporated within its *genre* the bourrée, the minuet and the dramatic idiom of the opera—resulting in the birth of the biblical oratorio, with its recitatives, arias and massive chorus effects. And it was sarcastically said of Dr. Greene's compositions that his secular music smelt of the church and his anthems of the theatre.

The Birth of the Oratorio

What factors led to the birth of the English oratorio? It is known that Handel himself performed in 1718 the Masque, *Haman and Mordecai,* within the sacred setting of the Duke of Chandos's Chapel at Cannons. And it is known too that Bernard Gates, the Master of the Children, performed in 1732 part of the same work at his Westminster residence before the composer as a surprise birthday present. On this occasion, the Children of the Chapel Royal were dressed in theatrical attire, and both dramatic action and stage scenery were used. In the same year of this performance Handel revised the music and altered its name to *Esther.* But it is still a matter of conjecture whether it was the Bishop of London's prohibition of the Children appearing in theatrical costume which led Handel to convert a work intended for the stage into a concert production 'in still life.' This was indeed by far the most practical and economical means of performance.

Handel's oratorios were immensely popular, so much so that the Precentor of York Minster noticed that their popularity had spread from London to almost every market-town in England. The *Messiah* is undoubtedly a contemplative work, wherein the audience meditates first upon the prophecies foretelling the advent of the Messiah; secondly, upon the sufferings and death of Christ; and finally upon the joy of His resurrection. And Handel himself once remarked, 'I did think I did see all heaven before me, and the great God Himself!'

The composer's love for pictorialism is evident in the chromatic theme of darkness, the shepherds' music in the Pastoral Symphony, the fluttering broken chords of the descent of the angelic hosts, the *coloratura* in 'His yoke is easy,' and the sighing motives in 'He was despised.' A mood of sadness is achieved through the frequent use of minor keys, as can be seen in The Overture with its theme of darkness later replaced by that of light. The composer's handling of texts reaches perfection in the numerous recitatives, e.g. 'Thy rebuke hath broken His heart' and 'For behold darkness shall cover the earth.'

The 'Dry Recitative' is quickly moving and normally accompanied by punctuating chords on a harpsichord. This form of recitative is invaluable to the composer that wants to expedite the dramatic narratives, because it is easily adaptable to sudden changes of thought and emotion, e.g. 'Behold, a virgin shall conceive.' But the 'Instrumental Recitative' transfers interest from the dramatic to the musical side; and the soloist no longer has the same rhythmical licence, or else he would throw the orchestra into chaos, e.g. 'Thy rebuke hath broken His heart.'

Another product of this century was the vocal solo called Aria ('Air'), which is divided into three sections: the middle one is set in contrast to the first and final sections, which have the same music. Thus in musical scores this final section is not always printed, instead the term *Da Capo* ('from the beginning') is inserted at the end of the middle movement, e.g. 'The trumpet shall sound.' The instrumental accompaniment of oratorios is perhaps the nearest approach in England towards the symphonic church music of the Viennese composers. Moreover, the accompaniment of the *Messiah* is based on the strings, with flutes and bassoons and oboes as optional extras. The trumpets and drums were reserved for the major climaxes, which sometimes were enriched by the organ. The continuo section consisted of the cello, the double-bass and the harpsichord.

Handel was not the only eighteenth-century composer to write oratorios in England, since there exists Thomas Arne's *Abel* (1744) and *Judith* (1761), William Boyce's *David's Lamentation over Saul and Jonathan* (1736) and *Solomon* (1743), William Crotch's *The Captivity of Judah* (1789) and *Palestine* (1812), and Maurice Greene's *The Song of Deborah and Barak* (1732). All these musicians were more inclined to set to music the blood and thunder stories of the Old Testament rather than the scenes from our Lord's life.

Whereas the people of Leipzig went to hear Bach's *Passions* in the sacred buildings of their churches, the people of London preferred to meditate upon our Lord's Passion within the more secular and comfortable surroundings of the Covent Garden and the King's theatres.

The Age of Festivals

This period saw the rise of non-liturgical musical performances. And the year 1724 witnessed the first meeting of the Three Choirs Festival 'for the benefit of the widows and orphans of the clergy of the three dioceses,' which combined the cathedral choirs of Hereford, Worcester and Gloucester. Other festivals were held in Birmingham and Norwich; and the greatest of all were the monster Handel Commemorations held in Westminster Abbey, of which the first in 1784 was graced with the presence of King George III. Seating was provided for an audience of almost three thousand; and there were an enormous choir of 275 singers and an orchestra of 249 players. The public performances of Handel's music did much to establish the English tradition of large amateur choirs.

Congregational Psalmody

An emphasis upon congregational participation in worship resulted in more frequent use of metrical psalm-singing within the Anglican Church, as well as in the introduction of hymn-singing within the Independent Churches. If metrical psalm-singing has never formed an essential part of *The Book of Common Prayer,* permission for its use was granted by Queen Elizabeth in 1559:

For the comforting of such that delight in music at the beginning, or in the end of Common Prayers, either at morning or evening, there may be sung an hymn, or such-like song, to the praise of Almighty God, in the best sorts of melody and music that may be conveniently devised, having respect that the sense of the hymn may be understood and perceived.

Between the years 1660 and 1860 many hundreds of metrical-psalters were published for the needs of the ordinary congregation. One of the most popular editions was undoubtedly Henry Playford's *The Divine Companion* (1701), that contained six psalm-tunes by John Blow and twelve hymn-tunes by Jeremiah Clarke, William Croft and others.

The Birth of Modern Hymnody

It was an Independent Minister, Isaac Watts (1674–1748), who created the modern hymn structure by borrowing the existing metres of metrical psalmody. His *Hymns and Spiritual Songs* (1707) included 'Come, let us join our cheerful songs,' 'When I survey the wondrous Cross' and 'Give us the wings of faith' (Second Edition, 1709). Watts supplied an even greater need with the *Divine and Moral Songs for Children* (1715), wherein appeared his lovely 'Cradle Song' (OBC 130). But his finest hymns were the paraphrases founded upon the old psalm-tune metres, e.g. 'From all that dwell,' 'Jesus shall reign' and 'O God, our help in ages past.' Another minister, Philip Doddridge (1702–51), wrote hymns upon the themes of his sermons for the benefit of his congregation and students at Northampton, where he was the Director of the Dissenting Academy, e.g. 'Hark the glad sound' (Luke 4:18–19). 'O God of Bethel' (Genesis 28:20–22) and 'Ye servants of the Lord' (Luke 12:35–8).

Methodism was certainly born in song and started as a movement within the Evangelical wing of the Anglican Church. Its hymns upheld the doctrines and the sacramental beliefs of the Established Church, although John Wesley was very much influenced by the Moravian tradition of hymnody in his earlier days. And with his brother Charles, he edited the Large Hymn Book—*A Collection of Hymns for the Use of the People called Methodists* (1780), which was modelled upon the requirements of the liturgy and intended to be a companion to the already existing hymn books of eucharistic and festal hymns, as well as to *The Book of Common Prayer*, which is centred upon the Calendar of the Christian Year:

> My chief wish and aim have been to supply such subjects to their respective seasons, as either, in an obvious or prophetic sense, relate to the history of man's redemption. I have profited in the choice of some subjects by the ancient custom of singing the Introits, which were psalms appointed for each Sunday or Holy Day, and on some account rendered proper for the day by their containing something prophetical of the evangelical history.

The Wesley brothers knew that hymns were the best way for teaching people to remember the basic doctrines of their Faith; hence John Wesley's description of the Large Hymn Book as 'a little body of experimental and practical divinity.' Further, every hymn in this collection had a place in the soul's pilgrimage through his earthly life that is seen in the Table of Contents. Part Four, for instance, was intended for Believers Rejoicing, Fighting, Praying, Watching, Working, Suffering, Seeking for full Redemption, Saved and Interceding for the World. And many hymn books borrowed this idea of classification, but with more attention in Anglican books given to the Catechism, the Church, Saints' Days, Litanies and Mission.

Whereas John himself was better known for his translations of the German Pietistic hymns (e.g. 'Lo, God is here! Let us adore' and 'Thou hidden love of God'), his brother Charles was indeed a prolific writer of hymns which all possess a warmth of friendliness and evangelical piety about them. His best known hymns include: 'Christ, whose glory fills the skies,' 'Come, Thou long-expected Jesus,' 'Come, O thou Traveller unknown' (based upon Genesis 32), 'Hail the day that sees Him rise,' 'Hark, how all the welkin rings,' 'Forth in Thy name, O Lord, I go' (for Believers before Work), 'Jesu, Lover of my soul,' 'Let saints on earth in concert sing' (for a funeral), 'Love divine, all loves excelling' (in imitation of Dryden's poem, *Fairest isle, all isles excelling,* which had already been set to music by Henry Purcell), 'O for a thousand tongues to sing' (written to commemorate the anniversary of his conversion), 'O Thou who camest from above' (paraphrased from a passage in Matthew Henry's *Commentary* on Leviticus 6 : 13), 'Rejoice, the Lord is King!' and 'Soldiers of Christ, arise' (for Confirmation).

Charles Wesley's hymns were very much indebted to Anglican beliefs and practices. His Trinitarian hymns were written for a defence against Unitarianism, e.g. 'Father, in whom we live' and 'Hail! holy, holy, holy Lord!' And his hymns contain many ideas from the Greek Church, such as the divinization of the soul and the concept of the double *epiklesis*: the coming of the Holy Spirit both upon the faithful and upon the bread and wine in the Holy Communion. And there is the Evangelical insistence upon conversion and the pursuit of perfection, as well as on the need for daily meditation and reading of the Bible:

When quiet in my house I sit,
   Thy Book be my companion still,
My joy thy sayings to repeat . . .

Moreover, John Wesley edited the *Hymns on the Lord's Supper* (1745) that included 166 hymns and an abridged version of Dean Brevint of Lincoln's *The Christian Sacrament and Sacrifice* (1673). Under this heading come the following hymns: 'Author of life divine' (A Sign and Means of Grace), 'Sons of God, triumphant rise' (Post-Communion Hymn), 'Summoned my labour to renew' (Offertory) and 'Victim Divine, Thy grace we claim' (Linked with the Sacrifice of Christ). So there is much eucharistic teaching in Methodism that is common to Anglican teaching.

Joseph Addison, the famous essayist, published in 1712 several fine hymns in *The Spectator:* 'The Lord my pasture shall prepare,' 'The spacious firmament on high' and 'When all Thy mercies, O my God.' And because hymns were not allowed in the liturgy of the Anglican Church, two Evangelicals (William Cowper and John Newton) published their *Olney Hymns* (1779) so that they could be sung at the prayer meetings held in Lord Dartmouth's Great Hall—hence the significance of Cowper's hymn, 'Jesus, where'er Thy people meet.' It is a pity that Newton's well-known hymn, 'Glorious things of Thee are spoken' is not sung more often during the Offertory in the Communion Service, for the following lines come in verse form, now omitted from modern hymn-books:

And as priests, His solemn praises
Each for a thank-off'ring brings.

The typical musical structure of our hymns is derived from the eighteenth-century dance forms of the Bourrée and the Minuet; that is to say, they were written in strict four-time or three-time, but with the main emphasis placed upon the first beat in the bar. And there was a variety of feeling to be experienced between the robust tunes of Croft's *Hanover* and *St. Matthew* and the stately melodies of Boyce's *Chapel Royal* and *Halton Holgate.* Nevertheless, the Handelian desire for good melodies resulted in an impoverishment of correct verbal rhythms sometimes in our hymns.

Three of Handel's hymn-tunes were discovered by Samuel Wesley in 1826 and are now in the keeping of the Fitzwilliam Museum at Cambridge. They were written at the request of Charles Wesley and were called *Cannons* (after the name of the London home of the Duke of Chandos, who was Handel's patron), *Desiring to Love* and *Gopsal* (from the name of the Leicestershire house of the Reverend Charles Jennens, who was responsible for the libretto of the *Messiah*).

This same period witnessed the marriage of many hymns to foreign tunes from three sources:

(i) German Chorales and Sacred Songs (e.g. *Eisenach, Innsbruck, Passion Chorale, Vulpius, Laus Deo, Nicht so taurig*).

(ii) French Diocesan Melodies (e.g. *Ave Radix Jesse, Christe Fons Jugis, Christe Sanctorum, Coelites Plaudant, Diva Servatrix, Iste Confessor, Regnator Orbis, Solemnis Haec Festivitas*).

(iii) Roman Catholic Embassies in London (e.g. *Melcombe, Tantum Ergo* and *Veni Sancte Spiritus* which all came from Samuel Webbe's *Motets and Antiphons* (1792); and the well-known tunes, *Adeste Fideles* and *St. Thomas* were composed by J. F. Wade (1711–86), who was a music copyist at Douai).

The Charity Children

The eighteenth century saw the building of several charity institutions, such as the Foundling Hospital (1738), the Lock Hospital (1746), and the Magdalen Hospital (1758). And the organists of these places published collections of hymn-tunes and other suitable church music for the benefit of the children. For example, the *Collection of Psalms and Hymns* (1760) was published by the Founder of the Lock Hospital, Martin Madan.[1]

It is not very often realized how much Handel has assisted the Foundling Hospital, both financially and musically. He wrote *The Foundling Anthem* (H) for a special concert in the chapel (1749); he later presented the chapel with a fine organ and gave many performances of the *Messiah*, which alone have contributed £10,000 towards work among children. At this same Hospital were printed *Psalms, Hymns and Anthems: Used in the Chapel of the Hospital for the Maintenance & Education of Exposed and Deserted Young*

[1] Martin Madan (1725–90) came very much under the influence of John Wesley, having been also ordained in the Anglican Church. Two editions of his popular *Collection of Psalms and Hymns* were printed in 1769 and 1792. From the first edition came the tune, *Moscow* (AMR 266) by Felice Giardini, a former chorister at Milan Cathedral; and from the second came the tune, *Carlisle* (AMR 362) by Charles Lockhart, the blind organist at the Lock Hospital Chapel.

Children (1774), in which appeared the well-known hymns: *Spirit of mercy, truth and love* and *Praise the Lord! ye heavens, adore Him,* which came in the second edition (1809) and is set to Haydn's *Austrian Hymn* by William Russell, the Hospital organist.

The Gallery Minstrels

They were drawn from the village folk and formed a colourful sight on Sundays, with their white smocks, buckskin breeches and yellow stockings; and with the ladies wearing red cloaks and white poke-bonnets. And, in spite of little heating in winter, hard-backed pews, stone floors and no hassocks, church attendance was popular throughout the country. Further, there were many indications of warmth and life about village worship, in which the congregation sat listening to the minstrels playing on their fiddles, flutes, charinets, 'cellos, bassoons, and perhaps even on a banjo or concertina! Their leader stood with his back to them, facing the congregation, as portrayed in Webster's famous painting, *A Village Choir* (1846). And whenever the band played, the congregation would turn to face the singing-loft until the metrical psalm was finished.

Although there were no hymns, the congregation fitted the words to the psalm-tunes as best they could, or remained silent. Their efforts at this are best described by Thomas Mace, who wrote in 1676: 'It is sad to hear what whining, yelling and screeching there is in many congregations, as if the people were affrighted or distracted.'

Composers of the Times

WILLIAM CROFT (1678–1727) held several important positions including that of a Gentleman of the Chapel Royal, Master of the Children and Organist to the Chapel, having shared this position with Jeremiah Clarke for three years. However, he succeeded his Master, Dr. Blow, as the organist of Westminster Abbey (1708–27).

Croft's music is dignified, but without being in any way dull. 'His emotions are always under control, as befits the eighteenth century scholar and gentleman; but in the long roll of English church musicians there are very few who are more deserving of our sincere and cordial respect' (Ernest Walker). His hymn-tunes are bold and stately; and many congregations must have enjoyed the swing belonging to the triple-measure of his tune *Hanover*. To the second edition of Henry Playford's *The Divine Companion* (1707) he contributed the tunes: *Croft's 148th*, *Binchester* and *Eatington*. And some of the anonymous tunes in the *Supplement to the New Version* (1708) were certainly by him, e.g. *Hanover*, *St. Anne* and *St. Matthew*.

In 1724 John Walsh published Croft's *Musica Sacra*, which included his beautiful and simple setting of *The Burial Service in G Minor* (N). Croft wrote this work to complete Purcell's *Thou knowest, Lord*, which he had included in the Appendix to his *Musica Sacra*. Croft also wrote a fine *Morning Service* in A (N), as well as many anthems which commemorated the frequent victories gained by the Duke of Marlborough.

MAURICE GREENE (1695–1755). The son of a London clergyman, he became a chorister at St. Paul's Cathedral and later its organist at the early age of twenty-three. In 1727 he succeeded Dr. Croft as organist and Composer to the Chapel Royal under George II. His *Forty Select Anthems* were published in the same year, being distinctive both for their dignified and massive style. From the year 1750, Maurice Greene lived on an estate inherited from a cousin, where he spent the remainder of his life in collecting English Cathedral Music. In the words of Charles Burney:

> Greene's figure was below the common size and he had the misfortune to be very much deformed; yet his manners were those of a man of the world—mild, attentive and well-bred. . . . It was sarcastically said, during the life of this composer, that his secular music smelt of the church, and his anthems of the theatre.[2]

[2] From *A General History of Music*, pages 489 and 491.

Greene was undoubtedly a versatile composer, with a wide range of expression, particularly seen in his full anthems: *O clap your hands* (N), *Lord, how long wilt Thou be angry?* (OUP), and *Lord, let me know mine end* (OUP), with its figured bass and treble duet, 'For man walketh in a vain shadow.' This last work was composed for Lord Nelson's funeral in St. Paul's and explains the sad chromaticism of the final bars—'And be no more seen.' Pictorialism is seen in his anthem, *God is our hope* (N), with its dramatic touches—'Though the earth tremble' and 'The waters rage and swell.' And there are the fine movements to his verse-anthems: 'I will lay me down' (from *O God of my righteousness* (N)), 'The Gentiles shall come' and 'The sun shall be no more' (from *Arise, shine, O Zion* (OUP)). Both Greene and Boyce were instrumental in establishing the full-scale cathedral anthem in England by adopting the cantata-like idiom of many movements for chorus and solo singing.

Greene also wrote a *Service in G* (CMS) and *Six Modal Anthems* (FP).

JOHN TRAVERS (1703–58) was a chorister at St. George's Chapel, Windsor. He was appointed organist of the Chapel Royal in 1737. And he composed an extended anthem, *Ascribe unto the Lord* (N), which is an excellent example of dramatic, if not operatic, music with its tenor recitative and lengthy baritone solo, 'Let the heavens rejoice,' and arresting chorus 'For He cometh to judge the earth.' Travers also wrote a Morning and Evening Service in F (N).

WILLIAM BOYCE (1710–79), the son of a Beadle to the Worshipful Company of Joiners, was a chorister and studied at St. Paul's Cathedral under Dr. Greene. Afterwards he was the organist at St. Michael's, Cornhill, and at the Chapel Royal after the death of John Travers in 1758. Besides being Master of the King's Band, he was one of the conductors at the Three Choirs Festival of 1737, where he was said to have used a roll of parchment in order 'to mark the measure' to the orchestra—indicating that it was unusual to employ a conductor's baton at this time.

He was one of our leading church musicians, whose hymn-tunes were distinctive for their dignity, flexibility and absence of florid harmonies, e.g. *Boyce, Chapel Royal, Halton Holgate* and *Kingsland*. Of his sixty or so anthems, the fine *O where shall wisdom be found?* (N) is remarkable for its vivid pictorialism (*weighed*), its flowing duet 'No mention shall be made of coral, or of pearls,' and for the traumatic chord of D flat at the word 'Lightning' in the minuet movement. An equally exciting work is the anthem, *The heavens declare the glory of God* (OUP) with its descriptive bass solo, 'Which *cometh forth* as a bridegroom . . . and *rejoiceth* as a giant to *run* his course,' and fine chorus 'Great and marvellous are Thy works.'

Boyce composed two Morning Services in A and C (N) and edited in three volumes an entire collection of *Cathedral Music* (1760–1778).

JOHN STANLEY (1713–86) lost his sight in early childhood by falling on a marble hearth. Yet this disability did not stop him studying music under Dr. Greene and afterwards being appointed organist at the Temple Church in 1734. He was without any doubt one of the best organists in the country; even Handel used to go and hear his final voluntary on Sundays. His *Voluntaries* (H) are remarkable for their brightness and rhythmical movement.

JAMES NARES (1715–83), a Child of the Chapel Royal, was appointed organist at York Minster (1734), where he made his reputation as a recitalist and a composer. He wrote the first instruction manual on harpsichord and organ-playing in 1759, besides the *Service in F* (N) and *Twenty Anthems in Score* (1778), about which he wrote : 'I have had the greatest regard to the words, endeavouring rather to illustrate their beauties and enforce their sentiments, than to display the art of musical composition.' His poular anthem, *The souls of the righteous* (N) is an extended work for experienced treble soloists and chorus.

The Barrel Organ

The hand-organ came into existence about 1772 in village churches and replaced the Gallery Bands. At the end of the century, Charles Burney noticed that mechanical improvements had made the barrel capable of playing music as well as 'the fingers of the first-class performers.' Many barrels contained not merely popular psalms and hymn-tunes, but music for the Anglican Chant with embroidered shakes that added further brilliance to the melody.

The eighteenth century witnessed the synthesis of sacred and secular styles in church music. The anthem was characteristic for its length (200–350 bars), its middle section for solo voices set in the style of a minuet, and its final section sometimes in fugal form. 'It is amazing to think,' writes Watkins Shaw, 'that the eighteenth century did not produce one really good cantata-style setting of the Canticles, doing for the English liturgy what the continental composers of the Mass were doing for the Roman rite. In our liturgical music, the grave, classic beauty of Croft's *Burial Service* stands apart.'

VI. *The Victorian Age and the Renaissance in Church Music*

'The Church as it now stands, no human power can save.'
So the Headmaster of Rugby, Thomas Arnold, wrote in
1832. And seventeen years later, while he was organist at
Leeds Parish Church, S. S. Wesley observed that Cathedral
Music, when compared with the well-regulated performances
elsewhere, bore to them about the proportion of life and
order which an expiring rush-light did to a summer's sun.
He was gloomy at the average Chapter's inability to effect
reforms from within, and wrote:

> Painful and dangerous is the position of a young
> musician who, after acquiring knowledge of his art in
> the Metropolis, joins a country Cathedral. At first he
> can scarcely believe that the mass of error and inferiority
> in which he has to participate is habitual and irre-
> mediable. He thinks he will reform matters, gently,
> without giving offence; but he soon discovers that it is
> his approbation and not his service that is needed.[1]

But a wind of change was blowing throughout the Church
of England. Thomas Arnold published his *Principles of
Church Reform* (1833); and the Ecclesiastical Commission
was permanently established three years later. Included in its
agenda was the reduction of cathedral staffs, involving the
curtailing of several Minor Canonries—particularly that of
the Precentor. Here Wesley entered the battle and endeavoured to put forward some urgent reforms in the Choral
Service, demanding at the same time well-trained singers,

[1] From *A Few Words on Cathedral Music and the Musical System of
the Church with a Plan of Reform* by S. S. Wesley (Leeds, 1849; Hinrichsen, 1965), pages 11 and 41.

the guidance of a Precentor, and Church Music of the highest standard. And he even went as far as suggesting some of the recent revolutionary findings of Leslie Paul's report, *The Deployment and Payment of the Clergy*:

> Multiplication of small uninteresting churches in the outskirts of large towns, however good in intention, is far from a universal success. Numerous instances occur in which churches are almost empty or the very next thing to it. One magnificent cathedral or church in a large town, with its musical services *properly* performed, would more surely attract a congregation of ten thousand than ten small churches of the ordinary kind, with a preacher as the sole attraction.[1]

Moreover, he demanded at least twelve lay-clerks with a stipend of £85 per annum and with compulsory attendance at rehearsals, the founding of a Musical College for the training of future organists and choirmasters and the creation of Professorships for cathedral organists with a salary between £500 and £800 per annum. He advised, too, the establishment of a responsible Musical Commission for looking after the musical affairs of the Church of England generally.

Another reformer of Cathedral worship was Dr. John Jebb (1805–86), who castigated Westminster Abbey for its low musical standards and 'coldness, meagreness, and irreverence in the performance of the divine offices.' And he continued with these remarks:

> The Choir, till of late years wretchedly few in number, were permitted to perform their duties by deputy; and these were discharged in a manner which at best was barely tolerable, without life or energy. The Lessons were commonly read with the same degree of solemnity as the most ordinary document by a clerk in a Court of Law. The service was opened in a manner the most careless: no decent procession was made; and the

striking of a wretched clock was the signal for the beginning to race through the office.' [2]

By 1875 there were no full rehearsals at the Abbey; and in parish churches the introduction of the harmonium [3] dispensed with the Gallery Musicians of the previous century. Furthermore, Stanford complained at the limited repertory of cathedral and collegiate churches.

A wind of change began to blow through our English cathedrals. It was musicians like Goss, Wesley, Walmisley, Stainer, Parry and Stanford who initiated reforms in the performance of the Cathedral Choral Service. And it was Maria Hackett (1783–1874) who led a personal crusade for the improvement of the moral and material welfare of choristers and to raise their general educational standards. She wrote *A Brief Account of Cathedral and Collegiate Schools* (1827).

The Cambridge Camden Society

It was founded in May 1839 through the initiative of two undergraduates, John Mason Neale (1819–66) and Benjamin Webb (1819–85).

As the Tractarians studied the writings of the Early Fathers, so the Camden Society delighted in exploring the Decorated Gothic churches of England, especially those belonging to the Middle Ages. All churches had to proclaim the basic sacramental truths of the Gospel; hence the nave, with its flanking aisles, signified the doctrine of the Blessed Trinity and the cruciform plan that of the Atonement. A clear-cut division was necessary between the nave and the chancel, with the latter further divided into sanctuary and choir. And it was J. M. Neale's idea that chancels should be raised by two or three steps, particularly where there were no screens.

[2] *The Choral Service of the United Church of England and Ireland* (1843), pages 132ff.
[3] The introduction of the harmonium in Europe was due to C. G. Kratzenstein (b. 1723) of Copenhagen, and to both G. J. Grenié (1756–1837) and A. F. Debain (1809–77) of Paris.

A similar idea was borrowed for the liturgical arrangement of sanctuaries, which were raised by three flights of three steps, making the altar the main focal point of parish churches. And to enable congregations to adore the Holy of Holies, pews were designed as low as possible. The correct position for the officiating clergy was in the chancel for the Offices; but the Lessons were read from an eagle-lectern placed in the nave, on the right side of the chancel arch opposite to the pulpit. The Litany Desk was set below the chancel steps in full view of the congregation.

The ecclesiologists showed little understanding of congregational worship. The people in the nave were merely spectators of the divine mysteries which were performed aloft. Neale himself had assigned the choir to a place in the west gallery ('flying pues'); he was not keen on the idea of singers seated in the chancel.

The Anglican Church owes a tremendous debt to the beliefs of the Camden Society. In the words of Professor Owen Chadwick:

> It was another part of that almost universal turning from the head towards the heart. Its roots lay in the desire to turn the churches into houses of prayer and devotion, where men would let their hearts go outward and upward in worship, instead of preaching-houses where their minds would be argued into an assent to creeds or to moral duties. The desire that all things done in church should be done decently could not stay confined to the architecture. It must affect also the appurtenances and ornaments, the methods of conducting the service. The restorers, influenced by the Romantic revival, looked to the medieval centuries to guide them. They were rebuilding chancels, favouring pointed arches, advocating frescoes instead of whitewashed walls. Inevitably, and without any leap of transition, they looked to the antiquarian precedent to teach them how to restore the dignity of worship.[4]

[4] *The Mind of the Oxford Movement*, pages 55–6.

Dr. Theodore Farquhar Hook was appointed Vicar of Leeds in 1837. Faced with a large industrial city and a parish which was spiritually dead as the dodo, the new Vicar had the medieval-planned church demolished and set about the erection of a new building, suitable for the liturgical needs of a large city. And it was to exemplify the basic principles of the Camden Society by having three liturgical units of nave, chancel and sanctuary, but with the last two units separated from each other by a large flight of steps.

Nevertheless, there were two departures in this Leeds plan : firstly, provision had been made for the communicants to come up at the time of the Invitation to kneel on the wide step next to the communion-rails; secondly, a surpliced and paid choir of lay clerks and boys were allowed to sit in the chancel—an innovation due to the influence of his musical friend, John Jebb, who maintained :

> In the constitution of her choirs the Church of England has made the nearest possible approach to a primitive and heavenly pattern. Her white-robed companies of men and boys, stationed at each side of her chancels, midway between the porch and the altar, stand daily ministering the service of prayer and thanksgiving.[5]

This arrangement proved unsuitable for many parish churches that copied Leeds. Whereas the services were fully choral there, many churches throughout the country would have had only said Communion Services, thus leaving an empty space between the celebrant in the sanctuary and the congregation in the nave. In fact, most medieval chancels were not designed to accommodate rows of choir-stalls and large organ-cases.

The Anglican Chant and Pointing of Psalms

The Anglican Chant is derived from the Gregorian tones

[5] *Three Lectures on the Cathedral Service of the Church of England* (1845), page 109.

which were harmonized by English composers during the sixteenth and seventeenth centuries. A good example is the *Tonus Peregrinus* Chant. Thus it became evident that the different numbers of syllables to each line could be easily accommodated by means of the reciting-note technique. Whereas the chants of the Restoration period were usually transcribed from the Gregorian tones, the seventeenth century saw the composing of new chants for the Anglican Service. If the eighteenth century chant was too ornamented like the *reports* styles in metrical psalmody, the nineteenth-century chant inclined towards sentimental chromaticism.

The introduction of systematic pointing to Anglican churches cannot be exactly dated. But the colon in the Prayer Book Psalter must have certainly marked a short pause in the singing. The choirmaster would have no doubt inserted the pointing-marks of the more difficult verses into his own copy beforehand. By the beginning of the nineteenth century the antiphonal chanting of the psalms in harmony was practised in most of our cathedrals. And it was the rise of the Oxford Movement that resulted in the full cathedral choral service being extended to the bigger town churches, thus making the Anglican Chant an essential part of Victorian worship.

In 1875, *The Cathedral Psalter* was printed and used in St. Paul's, whose choir seems to have been 'the guinea-pig' for other experiments in Anglican singing. The editor was Sir John Stainer, who encouraged a debased system of pointing through the sandwiching of too many words into the straitjacketed barring of the chant. An improvement was effected in Edward Hopkins' *The Temple Psalter* (1883).

The Authorization of Hymns

In 1819 the Reverend Thomas Cotterill imposed on his evangelical congregation at St. Paul's, Sheffield, a new hymn book, which was in fact a revised edition of *A Selection of Psalms and Hymns for Public and Private Use* (1810), published when he was the Vicar of Lane End in Staffordshire. This revised edition contained fifty hymns by the editor of *The Sheffield Iris,* James Montgomery, and also thirty-two by

Cotterill himself. The whole matter was then brought before the Diocesan Court at York, because hymns were then illegal in the public worship of the Church of England. However, it ended with the kindly intervention of Archbishop Vernon Harcourt, who suggested that the new hymn book should be withdrawn and that another edition, but this time approved by himself and dedicated to him, should be printed in 1820. Thus, by the beginning of the nineteenth century prejudice was dying out against the use of hymns in Anglican worship. The way was now clear for the publication of hymn books which would be assimilated within the pattern of worship as outlined in *The Book of Common Prayer*.

The Oxford Movement and Hymnody

This Movement (1833–45) extended its influence beyond the academic walls of Oxford to the more intimate atmosphere of country parish churches and vicarages. The earlier doctrinal emphasis on the historical Catholicity of the Church was soon transferred to that of worship and outward ceremonial, resulting in the Catholic Revival and the rebirth of Religious Life for women. Already Bishop Heber of Calcutta (d. 1826) had compiled his *Hymns written and adapted to the weekly Church Service of the year* (1827), in order 'to reinforce the lessons and the scheme of the Prayer Book' and to proclaim the missionary nature of the Church (viz. AMR 265). John Keble's *Christian Year* (1827) was undoubtedly the Bible of the Oxford Movement, consisting of a collection of religious verse for all Sundays and Feast Days of the Kalendar (AMR 4, 24, 154, 335); nor must one forget Henry Newman's *Dream of Gerontius* (1865) in which appeared the well-known hymns 'Firmly I believe' and 'Praise to the Holiest.'

By the middle of the nineteenth century, hymn-singing was an accomplished fact within the Church of England. And it was Benjamin Webb who persuaded J. M. Neale, the Warden of Sackville College, to undertake a collection of hymns translated from the Latin Office hymns and sequences, which would be sponsored by the Ecclesiological Society.

The result was *The Hymnal Noted,* published in 1852 (Part I) and 1854 (Part II), about which Neale wrote:

> The English being of course in the same metre as the Latin, no more alteration will be allowed in the melody than is permitted in the Latin books, between the different verses of the same hymn.

The musical editor was another priest, Thomas Helmore, who, in conjunction with Neale, published *Carols for Christmastide* (N, 1853) and *Carols for Eastertide* (N, 1854) that were based upon an ancient Swedish book, *Piae Cantiones* (FP).

A revival of plainsong was another product of the Oxford Movement. And Thomas Helmore, the first Precentor of the Gregorian Association, wrote a *Manual of Plainsong* (1850) and drew attention to the fact that plainsong would die in England unless there were an immediate revival:

> Through all the churches in the West, and in the unchanging East, we hear the traditional tones of Primitive Christian worship. Why should we in England presume to despise our own inheritance of the same and neglect, through want of enquiry, or reject, under the supercilious plea of superior taste and judgment, what they have with so great care and devout reverence treasured up in the past, and continually honour with more or less artistic skill in the present?

It was a chance meeting of two priests, W. Denton and F. H. Murray, in a railway carriage that led to the setting up of a committee in 1858, under the chairmanship of Sir H. W. Baker, that published the first edition of *Hymns Ancient and Modern* (1860, Music Edition 1861). And it was Mr. W. H. Monk, the first musical coadjutor, who suggested the suitable title of the book. *The Supplement* (1868) contained a hundred and fourteen new hymns, of which twenty-six were translations and some came from

Greek hymnody. Another eight new hymns were derived from Bishop Christopher Wordsworth's *Holy Year* (1862), including 'Gracious Spirit, Holy Ghost,' 'Hark! the sound of holy voices,' 'See the Conqueror mounts in triumph,' and 'Songs of thankfulness and praise.' Moreover, the Second Edition of *Hymns Ancient and Modern* (1875), containing four hundred and seventy-three hymns, was followed by another *Supplement* (1889) of one hundred and sixty-five hymns, edited by Charles Steggall.

The Victorian Age saw the writing of many hymns by bishops, deans, priests (some Roman Catholic), and by several notable women like the Irish-born Mrs. C. F. Alexander and the Worcestershire-born Miss F. R. Havergal. And the Victorian hymn-tune is distinctive for its friendliness and congregational singability: for example, Henry Smart's *Everton, Heathlands, Regent's Square* and *Rex Gloriae.* The leader of the Victorian School of hymn-tune writers was undoubtedly J. B. Dykes (1823–76), who was appointed the Precentor of Durham Cathedral. After his marriage in 1849 he moved to Hollingside Cottage, hence his tune *Hollingside.* The village of Horbury gave the name to another of his tunes:

> On June 1st, 1859, Dr. Dykes visited the Revd. John Sharp at Horbury and preached there. The special object of this visit was to make his first Confession. The hymn-tune which he named *Horbury* was written at this time; and it was to him a perpetual reminder of the peace and comfort he found then.

Dykes belonged essentially to the High Church Movement within the Church of England; and like J. M. Neale, he underwent much suffering due to a long and bitter conflict with his Diocesan, Charles Baring. A further tune was called after St. Oswald's Church, Durham, where Dykes was Vicar and where Professor Hutchings is now the organist. Dykes' tunes tended towards pictorialism, e.g. *Melita* and *St. Aelred,* and the rhetorical habit of too much note-repetition, e.g.

97

G

'the D-note complex' of *St. Oswald*. And it is interesting to compare the stateliness of *Alford, Gerontius, Melita, Nicaea* (cf. the tune *Watchet Auf*), and *St. Drostane* with the intimacy of the devotional atmosphere in *St. Bees, St. Cross* and *Dies Dominica*.

Another composer of hymn-tunes, W. H. Monk (1823–89) was responsible for many arrangements of foreign melodies like *Cruger, Wurtemberg* and *Victory* (adapted from Palestrina's setting of the Magnificat), as well as for fifteen new tunes in *Ancient and Modern* that display a definite freshness about them : for instance, *Evelyns, Menton, St. Bernard* and *St. Matthias*. Moreover, the following tunes are a fine example of Victorian hymnody: G. B. Elvey's *Diademata* and *St. George;* H. J. Gauntlett's *Gauntlett, Hawkhurst, Irby, St. Albinus* and *St. Fulbert;* G. A. Macfarren's *Dedication,* C. Steggall's *Christchurch* (cf. *Croft's 136th*) and *St. Edmund;* and A. Sullivan's *Lux Eoi.*

The saccharine chromaticism and sentimentality of the Victorian School of Barnby, Dykes and Stainer were replaced towards the end of the period by the bold melodies and stately harmonizations of both Parry and Harwood. And Stanford is best represented by his arrangements of the Irish tunes, e.g. *St. Columba* and *St. Patrick's Breastplate.*

Romanticism and Renaissance in Church Music

The nineteenth century was the age of the Gothic Revival, when the arts looked back to the past glory of the Middle Ages. In hymnody there was an antiquarian revival under Havergal, Helmore and Redhead that brought about a renewed interest in both plainsong and German tunes (compare AMR 48, 49, 50, 58, 142, 229, 250). And the Bristol-born Robert Lucas de Pearsall (d. 1856) settled in Germany, where he studied literary and archaeological subjects, besides his music which produced the well-known setting of *In dulci jubilo* (CFC 15) and two anthems in the ancient *conductus* style : *Blessed Word of God Incarnate* (CMS) and *Therefore we, before Him bending* (CMS).

Romanticism describes a movement in literature, art and

music affirming emotion and imagination in reaction from the classicism and rationalism of the eighteenth century. In England, S. T. Coleridge and W. Wordsworth wrote their *Lyrical Ballads* (1798); and the latter poet expressed his devotion to the Church of England in his *Ecclesiastical Sonnets* (1822). And in Germany the Romantic Age (1830–90) gave rise to choral and orchestral music associated with the names of Weber, Mendelssohn, Schumann and Wagner. Hence the advent of musical impressionism that placed a greater emphasis on the human imagination and the ability to portray the mood of texts in musical accompaniments.

But it was Mendelssohn and Brahms who most influenced English Church Music towards the end of the Victorian period. Mendelssohn conducted his oratorios *St. Paul* (1836) and *Elijah* (1846) in Birmingham and published *Six Organ Sonatas* (1845). And by 1880 English church music saw a renaissance effected by the choral music of Parry and Stanford, who were both admirers of Brahms' works.

Composers of the Victorian Age

THOMAS ATTWOOD (1765–1838), the son of a trumpet-playing coal merchant, became a Child of the Chapel Royal and later organist at St. Paul's Cathedral for over forty years. His music is full of beautiful melodies, but suffers from having too many four-beats-in-the-bar phrases. Of his anthems, the best known are *Come, Holy Ghost* (N), *Teach me, O Lord* (OUP) and *Turn Thy face from my sins* (N).

It has been held that Samuel Wesley (1766–1837), whose father was the famous hymn-writer Charles Wesley, was at his greatest when he had only voices to write for; this is certainly true of his fine Latin motets, *Exultate Deo* (N) and *In exitu Israel* (N).

WILLIAM CROTCH (1775–1847), the son of a Norwich carpenter, was certainly an infant prodigy. At fifteen he was appointed organist at Christ Church, Oxford, and later the Professor of Music in 1797. He had the honour of becoming the first Principal of the Royal Academy of Music in London

(1822). Crotch's music is clean-cut, but sadly dull, being too much influenced by the Handelian styles. He wrote two excellent oratorios: *The Captivity of Judah* (1789) and *Palestine* (1812), in which appeared the chorus *Lo, star-led chiefs* (N), a delightful anthem for Epiphanytide. And the best of his shorter anthems is undoubtedly *How dear are Thy counsels* (RSCM).

Of the anthems of Sir John Goss (1800-80) two are worthy of attention: *If we believe that Jesus died* (N) was composed for the State Funeral of the Duke of Wellington in 1852. It begins with a bold fugal entry in the bass part and finally modulates into the minor at the words 'Wherefore comfort one another.' And the next, *The Wilderness* (N), is a well-planned work, containing fine recitations and choir entries. Goss uses an organ accompaniment in the trio movement very similar to S. S. Wesley's treatment of the subject.

SAMUEL SEBASTIAN WESLEY (1810-76) undertook a cathedral pilgrimage, having been appointed organist of Hereford (1832), Exeter (1835), Winchester (1849) and Gloucester (1865). His music forms a bridge between that of Purcell and Stanford. He has left a *Cathedral Service in F* (N) and *Evening Service in E* (N), as well as many anthems marked by a dignified style and distinctive modulations. He delights in dramatic recitatives and arias, and also writes beautiful melodies: compare, for instance, the bass solo 'Say unto them that are of a fearful heart' from *The Wilderness* (N) and the soprano solo 'My voice shalt Thou hear betimes, O Lord' from *Praise the Lord* (AHC).

His use of discords and suspensions are ably shown in *Man that is born of a woman* (N), *O Lord, my God* (N), and *Wash me throughly from my wickedness* (N). Compare, too, the difficult chromatacism and the florid runs in his 'Thou judge of quick and dead' from *Let us lift up our heart* (AHC), which has been arranged for orchestra and choir by Sir Edward Elgar.

The organ accompaniment plays a vital part in Wesley's anthems, where it pictorially illustrates the texts, e.g. *The Wilderness,* with its stepping pedal-part and punctuating chords. Wesley is the first English composer to insert into his scores the exact directions as to what organ stops were to be employed.

Many of his anthems were written for special requirements and particular soloists. At the request of the Dean of Hereford, *Blessed be the God and Father* (N) was written for Easter Sunday 1833, and was for boys' voices and a bass soloist, who was none other than the Dean's butler! And the bass solo in *The Wilderness* was probably written for the bass voice of Mr. Penuel Cross, who was a lay-clerk of Winchester Cathedral. An amusing story lies behind Wesley's *Cast me not away* (N), which maintains that the anthem was written after the composer had broken his leg; hence the significance of the passage, 'The bones which Thou hast broken may rejoice.'

But the main defect in much of Wesley's music is the apparent inability to think of an anthem as a musical whole; instead he produces the Restoration type of miniature anthem that needs to be extended, e.g. *Thou wilt keep him in perfect peace* (Banks) and *The Lord is my shepherd* (N) where both the solo bass and treble parts are too short.

Being the grandson of the hymn-writer, Charles Wesley, it is no surprise to find him writing many original hymn-tunes, with new harmonic forms—yet taking care over the placing of his chords and not always having the melodic climax at the end, which was an established Victorian custom. His hymn-tunes include *Almsgiving, Aurelia, Brecknock, Colchester, Cornwall, Harewood, Hereford, Wigan* and *Wrestling Jacob.*

THOMAS ATTWOOD WALMISLEY (1814–56), the godson and pupil of Thomas Attwood, is chiefly remembered for his *Evening Canticles in D. Minor* (N, 1855) wherein the organ has an independent part—thus paving the way for Stanford's Services, and for his anthem *From all that dwell* (RSCM).

SIR FREDERICK ARTHUR GORE OUSELEY (1825–89), the son of the British Ambassador to Persia and Russia, was ordained to the priesthood in 1853 and was elected Professor of Music at Oxford two years later. In 1854 he laid the foundation stone of St. Michael's College, Tenbury. This was indeed a fulfilment of S. S. Wesley's hope for a college where the high standards in English Church Music would be maintained.

Ouseley wrote two oratorios, several Services and many anthems, helping to supply a need in Anglican music for more liturgical works for Festivals and Holy Week. *From the rising of the sun* (RSCM) is a buoyant work for Missionary Festivals, having an unusual ending, 'Thus saith the Lord.' And his Passiontide anthems, *Is it nothing to you?* (N) and *O Saviour of the world* (N) are Victorian church music at its best, displaying deep emotion without the intrusion of the organ. His finest hymn-tune is *Contemplation*.

SIR JOHN STAINER (1840–1901), the son of a schoolmaster, possessed high ideals of raising musical standards throughout England, which resulted in two important publications: *The Cathedral Psalter* (1875) and *The Cathedral Prayer Book* (1891), wherein he mutilated Merbecke's *Communion Service* through the harmonization of the plainsong and the introduction of bar-lines.

I saw the Lord (N) is an anthem for double choir, which contains repeated chords and a highly-rhythmical pedal-part in the organ accompaniment. The work is divided into three sections: the middle one ends abruptly at the word 'smoke,' and the final movement contains a scintillating melody that is first sung by the trebles.

Stainer's hymn-tunes are marked by their cheerful atmosphere: *Charity, Cross of Christ, In Memoriam, Love Divine, Scientia Salutis, St. Francis Xavier,* as well as in the more intimate tunes *Eucharistus, Sebaste* and *Vesper*.

SIR HUBERT PARRY (1848–1918) was heart and soul an Englishman. His choral music displays a nobility of spirit and a love for massive, dramatic effects, which are very much evident in the *Ode to a Solemn Music* (1887) and *I was glad* (N). Although Parry was an unbeliever, he is an excellent example of a secular composer being drawn into writing serious music for the Church. His abiding nationalism is seen in the song *Jerusalem*, which was written at Robert Bridges' suggestion and first performed in the Royal Albert Hall (1916). The oratorios *Judith* (1888) and *Job* (1892) were regularly sung at music festivals; and the psalm-setting *De Profundis* (1891) was given its first performance at the Three Choirs Festival in Hereford.

His elaborate anthem *Hear my words, ye people* (N) contains an interesting organ accompaniment, with sections for full choir, semi-chorus (i.e. the cathedral choir), and difficult solos for treble and bass voices—the latter has a highly dramatic passage, 'Clouds and darkness are round about Him.' Three years before he died, Parry began writing the *Songs of Farewell* (AHC). These anthems are extended compositions for unaccompanied singing, wherein Parry shows his skill at dramatic climaxes, e.g. 'Thy God, Thy life, Thy cure' (from *My soul, there is a country*).

He has written many fine hymn-tunes, including *Intercessor, Laudate Dominum, Repton* and *Rustington*.

SIR CHARLES STANFORD (1852–1924) came of Irish descent, and his music is influenced by folk song and is always open to the winds of romanticism: 'His Tennysonian spirit shows itself in his great partiality for words dealing with nature, especially the sea, or expressing the romantic side of patriotism' (Ernest Walker).[6] Stanford also introduced 'the symphonic approach' to English Church Music, which involved the repetition of certain musical motifs throughout a work, thus giving a unified effect—instead of a series of unconnected movements strung together as in the Restoration Anthem: for example, the theme of the *Coronation Te Deum in B Flat* (N, 1902) originated from Gregorian intonations and is repeated many times by the voices and the organ accompaniment, especially in the pedal-part. The

[6] From a *History of Music in England*, page 336.

vitality of this choral work is achieved through frequent modulation, alternating unison and contrapuntal singing, and through the staccato-effect in the pedal-part also assisted by the drums. And it is interesting to find a similarity between the final bars and those of Henry Smart's *Te Deum in F*.

The organ accompaniment has an important part to play in Stanford's Services, wherein the organ's thematic material is borrowed by the voices and then returned, just as one section of an orchestra imitates the melody played by another. And the organ helps to support the vocal parts, but without overloading the accompaniment with superfluous notes in what Herbert Howells has so aptly called 'the tonal elephantiosis encouraged by the misuse of outsize organs!' An excellent example of this economical use of the organ is seen in the *Gloria Patri* of Stanford's *Evening Service in C* (SB, 1909) where added spaciousness is effected through the ascending pedal part and the rests for the unaccompanied singing of the choir. But the most beautiful of his settings is undoubtedly the *Magnificat in G* (SB, 1902), where there is a flowing, if not lyrical, accompaniment portraying an Irish peasant's playing upon her lyre; together with the choir singing in the background, quietly meditating upon the passages of the treble soloist.

The 'symphonic' pattern is also seen in the anthem, *The Lord is my Shepherd* (N, 1886), in which the pastoral introduction is followed by an air of uneasiness in the organ accompaniment, in contrast to the sinister tones of the voices symbolizing the Valley of Darkness (bars 74–176). Again, the organ punctuates the bass and tenor parts of the middle movement, thus leading into the final section that is introduced by a lyrical treble passage, 'But Thy loving kindness and Thy mercy shall follow me all the days of my life.' An Easter anthem, *Ye choirs of New Jerusalem* (SB, 1911), also contains a flowing treble part and makes use of modulation to divide the work into its various movements. The full choir invades with an arresting section, 'For Judah's Lion burst His chains.' The contrapuntal middle section ends with a climax at 'Triumphant in His glory.' This exciting choral work ends with a set of flowing Alleluias.

Stanford's *Three Motets* (BH, 1905) must rank as one of his most imaginative works and equal to anything written by the Tudor composers. They were composed for Dr. Alan Gray and his choir at Trinity College, Cambridge, and were originally sung on Gaudy Days in the Hall. His oratorios include *The Three Holy Children* (1885), *Eden* (1897), *Requiem* (1897), and the fine *Stabat Mater* (1907).

The Victorian age was distinctive for its evangelical zeal—establishing family prayers, Sunday School anniversaries and the revival of Harvest Thanksgivings by the Revd. R. S. Hawker in his Cornish parish of Morwenstow in 1843. This same age also saw the introduction of the practice of evening communions for the working classes, besides the employment of unconsecrated buildings for religious worship.

Many colleges of music were founded for the benefit of those unable to afford an expensive university education, e.g. the Royal Academy of Music (1822), the Royal College of Organists (1865), and the Royal College of Music (1883). This period saw the birth of many musical societies, like the Bach Society (1849), the Purcell Society (1876) and the Plainsong and Medieval Music Society (1888). And in hymnody, two women collected and translated foreign hymns that were later printed in *Hymns Ancient and Modern.*[7]

There is much evidence to show that the Victorian clergyman and musician did endeavour to raise the standard of choral worship, in spite of S. S. Wesley's scathing criticisms of cathedral chapters. Between the years 1832 and 1834 Dr. John Jebb arranged his choir at Coleraine in college-fashion and dressed the choirboys in surplices, which their parents had made from inexpensive Irish linen. He became Vicar of Peterstow and a Prebendary of Hereford Cathedral in 1843, finding time to produce books about the choral service, responses and litanies that were sung in England and Ireland during the Tudor period. And he regarded the

[7] Frances Cox's *Sacred Hymns from the German* (1841–64) and Catherine Winkworth's *Chorale Book for England* (1863).

choral service as an ornament to the divine liturgy, but disparaged congregational singing in worship.

And it was through the vision and enthusiasm of Sir Frederick Bridge that a new Choir School was opened and regular rehearsals for lay-clerks and choristers were again held at Westminster Abbey. Also at the Temple Church, Dr. Edward Hopkins laid the foundation of the typical Victorian choral service. Moreover, Jebb noticed in 1843 that its choir was moved from the gallery into two sets of choir-stalls on each side of the church, 'so to exhibit both visibly and audibly the antiphonal nature of the service.' Hopkins was a notable choir-trainer and encouraged the correct pointing and verbal accentuation of the psalms, which can be seen in his editing of *The Temple Psalter* (1883).

The Victorian composer delighted in writing tuneful melodies and popular part-songs, rather than in using polyphony and folk-song.

VII. *The Age of Liturgical Reform and of Experimental Church Music*

Worship is our response to God's love through silence, prayer and praise. And in church music this activity is expressed in manifold forms: drama and dancing, singing and playing upon musical instruments. Indeed, every age and culture have made their mark on Christian worship; nowhere is this fact more apparent than in the church music of this century. The contemporary emphasis upon the doctrine of the Body of Christ has resulted in worship being regarded as the organic activity of the whole of God's people and not merely as a function for choir and clergy alone.

Furthermore, church architecture has never stood in isolation from the rest of the world. It has had in recent years to reconcile itself to the same rationalization that has been experienced in the realm of modern design—involving such matters as the control of atmosphere, light and sound. Some of our English parish churches have adopted the circular design, where both the communion-table and the pulpit form the main focal point, emphasizing the importance of both the Word and the Sacrament, as well as the idea of 'the gathered community.' What is noticeable is the complete absence of the apse and the choir departments. And the appearance of the nave-altar after the Second World War can be compared to 'the thrust stage' of the modern theatre. One has only to compare the Anglican Cathedral in Liverpool with the new Roman Catholic Cathedral of Christ the King to understand that church architecture has experienced a renaissance during the last twenty years.

Whereas the Victorian ecclesiologist held that the correct position for the surpliced choir was alone in the chancel, thus reinforcing the distinction between those who sing and those who do not, it is now evident that the best position for the choir is behind the congregation, although the siting of the organ must remain the decisive factor.

The Liturgical Movement

This catholic movement originated in France with the work of Dom Guéranger (1805–75), who restored the ruins of the Benedictine Abbey of Solesmes that had been destroyed in the French Revolution. Here the monks studied the ancient Greek liturgies and hymns, together with the plainsong chants which led to the restoration of the Gregorian Chant in the Daily Offices. This movement has quickly spread to other countries. At Klosterneuberg, in Austria, a considerable emphasis was given to the study of the Bible and the Liturgy; but it was the Belgian Benedictines that envisaged the Liturgy as the corporate activity of the whole Church and that parish worship must involve the laity's sharing in the prayers and the praises of the Mass, as well as in the offering of their daily work to God through the Offertory. Alongside this aspect of the movement went the idea of parish mission : that bringing of the people into the spirit of the Liturgy by means of the dialogue Mass, besides making them realize that salvation involves the saving of our modern society. And it was Pope Pius X who demanded that men must not sing or pray during the Mass, but that they must sing and pray the Mass.

It was Fr. Gabriel Hebert's book, *Liturgy and Society* (1935), that really began this movement in England. This Anglican monk maintained that the Church's function in this modern age was to redeem the pagan masses through the celebration of the Parish Eucharist :

> When we have learnt again to celebrate the Lord's Service thus—not as a devotional service for the inner circle of the faithful in the early morning, nor as a mid-morning act of devotion with no communicants except the priest, but making the Parish Eucharist with the communion of the people the central act of worship on

every Sunday—that service will teach us, by our participation in it, the meaning of the Fellowship of the Body more effectively than all our books of theology.

The Parish Eucharist

The first instance of this form of service in England was at Temple Balsall, in Warwickshire, as far back as 1913. And twenty-five years later, the Parish Eucharist was successfully initiated at the new John Keble Memorial Church on the Mill Hill estate, where the modern ideas of the Liturgical Movement were put to the test, with the choir placed in the front portion of the nave and the organ in the west gallery, in order to encourage full congregational participation.

This participation matters most of all and is achieved if the congregation is allowed to join in the Introit Psalm or Hymn, the Collect for Purity, and in the Prayer of Humble Access. The Epistle is best read from one of the excellent modern translations by a layman; and both the Creed and the Gloria should be said or sung to a familiar setting. The Offertory procession and the Intercessions, possibly read by a member of the congregation, will enhance this particular aspect of lay-participation—so will the insertion of appropriate responses after the main sections of the Prayer for the Church. The choir and people should be encouraged to join in the singing of the *Sanctus,* the *Agnus Dei* and the Communion hymn. The performance of a motet by the choir during the Communion of the people would be a fitting expression of their offering to God. The music of this Parish Eucharist should be simple and easy to learn, such as Patrick Appleford's *Mass of Five Melodies* (W), Merbecke's *Holy Communion* (OUP, edited by Arnold), Martin Shaw's *An Anglican Folk Mass* (C), and Sydney Nicholson's *Communion Service in C* (FP). But for churches with more experienced choirs, Kenneth Leighton's *Communion Service in D* (CMS) is excellent.

The Liturgical Commission

This Commission was set up in 1954. And, eleven years

later, the Church Assembly Prayer Book Measure was passed, resulting in the publication of the *Alternative Services* (SPCK). Whereas the First Series was a conservative revision by the bishops of *The Prayer Book as proposed in 1928,* the Second Series was an adventurous attempt at writing new services for our modern age by members of the Liturgical Commission. Conciseness is achieved in these new forms of the Daily Offices by the omission of superfluous directions, e.g. 'Let us pray,' 'Here beginneth,' etc., and by the avoidance of verbosity in the General Confession and the Absolution. The *Te Deum* and the *Benedictus* are transposed in order to emphasize the Incarnation, with the former now used as a hymn of praise, with its three sections permitted to be said separately. A rubric allows the preaching of a sermon at any part of the service. But no mention is made of places where hymns can be sung. Many Seasonal Sentences are provided, yet the Church of England has still to decide what nature the introduction to the Offices should take, whether penitential or seasonal.

Considerable flexibility is seen in the rubrics of *The Draft Order for Holy Communion* (1965) that permits the use of canticles, hymns and psalms. An anthem for the choir can be sung during the Communion of the people. Furthermore, the Offertory has been restored to its correct place before the Eucharistic Prayer; and nine subheadings replace the normal division between 'the Liturgy of the Word' and 'the Liturgy of the Upper Room.'

The last ten years has witnessed not only the publication of many translations of the Bible, such as *The New English Bible* and *The Jerusalem Bible,* but also the appearance of many liturgical studies on worship, including Patrick Cowley's *Advent* (FP), John Durham's *Directed Silence* (FP), John Robinson's *Liturgy Coming to Life* (Mowbray), E. C. Whitaker's *The Baptismal Liturgy* (FP) and Fr. Gelineau's erudite *Voices and Instruments in Christian Worship* (1964). The Parish and People Movement (1950) and the Institute for the Study of Worship and Religious Architecture at Birmingham University have already made their mark on Anglican public worship.

The spiritual value of the cathedral choral service has again been questioned in church circles. On the one hand, there are those Philistines who maintain that these sung services are irrelevant to the modern situation and form an expensive luxury to the esoteric few, if not a waste of the Church's limited finances that are needed for the missionary field and the training of candidates for the Ministry. On the other hand, Archbishop Lang pleaded in 1941 for the maintenance of cathedral music as one of the main duties and responsibilities of cathedral chapters. But it is morally wrong to regard the maintenance of high musical standards and liturgical ideals as a waste of money. The choral service must be seen as a sacrificial offering of man's talents, time and money in the service of God's kingdom on earth, just as the Woman of Bethany was commended by Christ for anointing His head with costly oil. Many choristers have experienced the life of the Anglican liturgy and have dedicated their lives to Christ's service—later becoming priests, church musicians and laymen well-grounded in the faith and the mystery of divine worship.

Furthermore, the cathedral is the mother church of the diocese, whose services are expected to be decently ordered and disciplined. But the Philistines are correct in demanding that what actually takes place within these ancient walls should be related to what is happening in our parishes. Liturgical worship has not only to be founded upon the past experience of tradition, but has also to serve the needs of the contemporary world; otherwise its worship would become fossilized and cut-off from the main stream of the Church's life, with no message to proclaim or mission to the world. Both flexibility and communication are the hall-marks of healthy worship. An example of this flexibility and readiness to serve mankind is seen in the disappearance of choral mattins from the Sunday menu of services in favour of the choral eucharist, which has been achieved at Bristol Cathedral.

Did not the Abbé Michenneau express the wish, 'Let the

Liturgy be splendid and full of meaning'? It is good to find Coventry Cathedral's commissioning exciting settings of the Communion Service, e.g. Adrian Cruft's *Mass for St. Michael* (BH), Brian Easdale's *Missa Coventrensis* (Chester), and William Walton's *Missa Brevis* (OUP).

Modern Psalmody

The last sixty years have seen the publication of many pointed-psalters, enabling both choirs and congregations to participate more fully in psalm-singing. One of the pioneers of reform in Anglican chanting was Robert Bridges, who in 1935 suggested that more rhythmic variation could be achieved by repeating the reciting note or the melody notes of the chant. Whereas the *Oxford Psalter* (1929) and the *Choral Psalter* (1957) have used the method of free-speech rhythm, the *Parish Psalter* (1928) has utilized both the *alla breve* (seven accents) and the *sapphic* (four accents) techniques of pointing.

A further step towards a uniformity of pointing throughout the Anglican Church came with the setting-up of the Archbishops' Commission to Revise the Psalter in 1958. It was to be a conservative revision, 'designed to remove obscurities and serious errors of translation, yet such as to retain, as far as possible, the general character in style and rhythm of Coverdale's version and its suitability for congregational use.' In 1963 the amended text was finally approved; and three years later the Pointed Psalter was published in the hope that it may lead to 'a uniform use in the Church of England.'

The Gelineau Psalms (Fontana Books, 1963) have become immensely popular in churches. This translation from *The Jerusalem Bible* (1950, English trans. 1966) was the inspired work of many scholars, whose aim was to retain the poetical rhythm and the verse structure of the Hebrew Psalms. And it was left to the ingenuity of Fr. Gelineau to devise a musical system whereby these psalms could be sung to the same rhythms. In England, the Grail initiated the making of two musical books, which contained between them fifty-four psalms and three canticles (1956–58), with the assistance of Dom Gregory Murray on the musical side. The main difference between this version and that of the *Revised Psalter* is that it is merely an excellent paraphrase, whereas the *Revised Psalter* is an accurate revision of the Coverdale Version in the light of modern biblical research. Nevertheless, the Gelineau method of psalm-singing has brought a breath of fresh air into modern worship and has caused Christians to reflect once more upon the message of the psalms.

Modern Hymnody

It was Robert Bridges who once referred to the modern hymn book as that which filled the sensitive worshipper with dismay, keeping some people away from church. And with him, men like Percy Dearmer and Vaughan Williams have all determined to raise the literary and the musical standards of our hymn books because they sincerely believed that this was a moral issue. Bridges himself has maintained that it is the mood of the hymn which must govern the tune as to whether it is suitable or not, 'for the enormous power that the tune has of enforcing or even creating a mood is the one invaluable thing of magnitude which overrides every other consideration.' Some earlier reforms in hymnody were effected first by the *Yattendon Hymnal* (1899), compiled by Robert Bridges for his village church in Berkshire, and next by *The Songs of Syon* (1910), which was essentially an antiquarian collection, edited by the Revd. G. R. Woodward with the assistance of Dr. Charles Wood.

The English Hymnal (1906, Second Edition 1933) marked an immense advance within our hymnody. And its green covers were at once a symbol of Anglo-Catholicism in parishes. Many bishops, including Charles Gore, objected to the doctrinal implications made in the book, such as the invocation of the saints. This partisanship was a pity, because the Preface maintained that the hymns of Christendom 'show more clearly than anything else that there is even now such a thing as the unity of the Spirit.' And concerning the musical standards of hymnody, the Musical Editor (Vaughan

113

H

Williams) had some strong opinions to make on the subject:

> It is indeed a moral rather than a musical issue. No
> doubt it requires a certain effort to tune oneself to the
> moral atmosphere implied by a fine melody; and it is far
> easier to dwell in the miasma of the languishing and
> sentimental hymn-tunes which so often disfigure our
> services. Such poverty of heart may not be uncommon,
> but at least it should not be encouraged by those who
> direct the services of the Church; it ought no longer to
> be true anywhere that the most exalted moments of a
> church-goer's week are associated with music that would
> not be tolerated in any place of secular entertainment.[1]

This book was infused by the spirit of secular, folk-song
melodies, e.g. *Agincourt Song, Capel, King's Lynn, Monk's
Gate, Royal Oak* (derived from 'The Twenty-ninth of May'
in *The Dancing Master* of 1686). And it contained fine
German and French psalm-tunes, which the Musical Editor
had adapted to the existing texts or simply had new words
written for them by Laurence Housman and Percy Dearmer.
As a matter of principle, he insisted upon congregational
singing and suggested that both the first verses of hymns
and their doxologies should be sung in unison.

Many fine hymn-tunes first appeared in this book, including *Cranham, Down Ampney, Randolph, Sheen* and
Sine Nomine, as well as several Welsh melodies like
Gwalchmai, Llanfair and *Rhuddlan* that was set to Scott
Holland's new hymn, 'Judge eternal.' Percy Dearmer himself contributed the well-known hymn 'Jesu, good above all
other' and the May Day Carol 'The winter's sleep,' as well
as the hymns: 'A brighter dawn,' 'Holy God, we offer here,'
and 'Lord, the wind and sea obey Thee.'

The English Hymnal Service Book (1962) indicated
another change in the pattern of Anglican liturgical life. It
was designed chiefly for use in the Parish Eucharist; therefore
it contained a table of Introit Psalms and Merbecke's setting

[1] From the Preface (*The Music* by R. Vaughan Williams) to *The
English Hymnal* (1906), by permission of the Oxford University Press.

of *The Holy Communion*. Moreover, the editors suggested that many more hymns should be used in this service: the Advent hymns might be sung before the Gospel, and the Easter hymns on Sundays just before the congregation dispersed after the Blessing. By containing the melodies of the Responses and a simple pointing of the Psalms of David, this book formed indeed a unique companion to the Prayer Book Services. Almost three hundred hymns were borrowed from *The English Hymnal* and thirty-seven carols and hymns were derived from other sources. This edition has many fine tunes, including *Affection, Fifer's Lane, Fudgie, Solothurn* and *Tredegar*.

Songs of Praise (1925, Second Edition 1931), called after James Montgomery's 'Songs of praise the angels sang,' was nothing less than an *avant-garde* national and religious songbook for schools and those congregations which inclined towards the teaching of modern liberalism. It was sponsored by Liverpool Cathedral, Dick Sheppard and the Evangelical Group Movement. Canon Dearmer endeavoured to improve the literary quality of the hymns by introducing poems by Coleridge, Hardy, Shakespeare, Shelly and Wordsworth. But he did discover a new hymn-writer in 'Jan Struther,' Mrs. Maxtone Graham, who contributed to the Enlarged Edition: 'Lord of all hopefulness,' 'Round the earth a messenger runs,' and 'When a knight won his spurs.'

The best part of this hymn book is undoubtedly the music, which is fresh and highly-rhythmical. This was due to the magnificent team-work of the brothers, Martin and Geoffrey Shaw, who had both played an important part in the raising of the musical standards at Canon Dearmer's parish church of St. Mary's, Primrose Hill, Hampstead. They were assisted by Vaughan Williams' researches into traditional folk-song melodies. The following tunes appeared for the first time in Anglican hymnody: Darke's *Cornhill*, Harris's *Alberta*, Ireland's *Love Unknown*, Martin Shaw's *Little Cornard* and *Marching*, Slater's *St. Botolph*, Vaughan Williams' *King's Weston* and *Marathon*, besides the arrangements of the Irish tunes: *Daniel, Slane* and *St. Sechnall*.

Hymns Ancient and Modern Revised (1950) was a conservative revision because the post-war period was unsuitable for revolutionary changes in hymnody. Sir Sydney Nicholson was the main figure behind this revision, as he had also been in the *Shortened Music Edition* (1939) wherein appeared his fine tune *Bow Brickhill*. And to this Revised Edition he contributed several tunes in a freely-rhythmical style, e.g. *Aethelwold, Leamington* and *St. Nicolas*. After his death in 1947, Canon Lowther Clarke was appointed the Chairman, but with the assistance of Dr. Gerald Knight and Dr. Dykes Bower on the musical side. The publication of this new hymn book was well received, although its hymn-tunes displayed a conservative idiom compared to some of the compositions in *Hymns for Church and School* (1964)—Eric Routley's adventurous *St. Augustine,* John Joubert's *Moseley,* John Gardner's *Ilfracombe,* Herbert Howells' *Salisbury* and *Sancta Civitas.* Nevertheless, many finely-constructed hymn-tunes did appear, as for instance: Blake's *Remission* and *Twyford;* Dykes Bower's *Amen Court, Elton* and *Standish;* Darke's *Naphill;* Harris's *Kybald Twychen, North Petherton* and *Sennen Cove;* Stanton's *Dolberrow;* Statham's *Arncliffe;* Cyril Taylor's *Abbot's Leigh* and *Belstead;* and Watson's *Stonor.* It is very encouraging to find two tunes composed by choristers: Jesson's *Barnet* and Symonds' *Mernle.*

The Anglican Hymn Book (1965) is a subjective collection of hymns for the Evangelical section of the Anglican Church, being faithful both to Scripture (with texts printed above each hymn) and to The Book of Common Prayer. There are eleven new hymns, including a paraphrase of *The New English Bible's* version of the Magnificat (439). But there is an immense poverty in Communion and Office hymns; and there has been too much mutilation of texts through the sub-editing of verses—thus avoiding their doctrinal implications. However, the great merit of this book is the assembling of hymn-tunes from other streams of hymnody and the supplying of the first bars of the melody of each tune in a unique metrical index. The music is excellent, even if the young editor, Robin Sheldon, has been not so ruthless as

Vaughan Williams was at the same age in the editing of *The English Hymnal.* There are forty-two new tunes, including Finlay's *Cobham* and *Glenfinlas;* Grundy's *Criggle-stone* and *Dumpton Gap;* Llewellyn's *Majesty* and *Tidings;* Richard Lloyd's *Sarum New;* Routley's *Varndean;* Sheldon's *Daymer* and *Jonathan;* Thalben-Ball's *Arden* and *Stand Up;* and finally David Willcocks' *Conquering Love.*

The Twentieth Century Light Music Group

This Group has brought a renewed vitality into the singing of hymns at family worship and at youth meetings. Since the first appearance of Father Beaumont's tunes, *Chesterton* and *Gracias* (Paxton, 1957), many collections of this Group's jazz hymn-tunes have been published by Weinberger, of which the following tunes are representative: Patrick Appleford's *Alton* and *Liverpool;* Geoffrey Beaumont's *Catherine, Cheerful, Higham Ferriers* and *Sunderland;* Michael Brierley's *Camberwell;* Peter Firth's *Forty Days;* John Glandfield's *Sons of the Living God;* and Frederick Parsonage's *Cooper* and *Gower-Jones.*

We have already referred to Patrick Appleford's *Mass of Five Melodies* (W). But it was Father Beaumont's *20th Century Folk Mass* (1956) that pioneered this kind of jazz-Mass, although his setting suffered from too much repetition by the congregation of the cantor's part. And Malcolm Williamson's *Mass of St. Andrew* (1964) also contained melodies in the style of the *palais de dance* quick-step, but is disappointing and dull compared to Appleford's Mass. It was due to the same Group's initiative that fifty-two new hymns (W) were written for the parish Mass in 1965.

Alongside this Group's activity, there have been published smaller collections of carols and satirical ballads, which have conveyed the Christian message in an arresting and original way, e.g. Sydney Carter's *9 Carols or Ballads* ('Lord of the Dance,' 'Friday Morning,' 'The Devil wore a Crucifix') and *10 New Songs* ('The Mask I wore,' 'The Rat Race'); and *New Hymns for A New Day* (*Risk*—Volume II, No. 3, 1966, published by the Youth Departments of the

World Council of Churches), which is the most comprehensive collection of modern hymns in this style to have appeared to-day.

But it must be remembered that hymns and spiritual songs form a valuable aid in the teaching of the Faith. They are, in fact, the only credal forms that ordinary people learn by heart; and it is vital that their texts should contain the theological insights of our age, by avoiding excessive sentimentality. And the musical Puritan, Charles Cleall, has many scathing remarks concerning the use of this kind of jazz music in church services:

> Have 'pops' a place in church? They draw: they reach the masses: but they do so because they are intrinsically barbarous; by which they shut man out of a knowledge of the beautiful. They try to raise themselves to the highest position in his life; that of the ideal: the pop-star is his God.[2]

This kind of musical dogmatism makes worship a bore, instead of making it a joyful and liberating experience that is shared between 'young men and maidens, old men and children' (Psalm 148). For the Church exists to serve people not ready to be brought into the centre of the worshipping community. As our Lord Himself used the common things in life to express divine truth, so the Church of our present age must use the medium of folk-song in order to communicate the Gospel message to those in desperate need of God's forgiveness. Indeed, the Church's mission has always extended itself beyond its own members to the uncultured and the uncommitted. Sacred music requires to be related to modern culture and life, or else it will become as fossilized as the dance music of the 1920s. There is clearly a place for the spiritual song in worship of a non-liturgical nature. The Archbishops' *Report* has confirmed that there is a place for the subjective in worship, adding that we must beware of starving emotion, remembering that there is room for the tender alongside with the robust.

[2] From *Music and Holiness* (Epworth Press), page 39.

The Royal School of Church Music

This is the largest musical foundation within the Anglican Communion. Its original name was The School of English Church Music, which was founded by Sir Sydney Nicholson in 1927. And the year 1945 marked the granting of a Royal Charter that gave the College its present name. Under the Director, Dr. Gerald Knight, the work of the R.S.C.M. has spanned the world, with a spectacular rise in the number of affiliated choirs from four thousand to almost eight thousand during the last twelve years.

The main aim of the R.S.C.M. has been to further the work and to uphold the standards of church music and public worship in the Anglican Communion, which has been achieved by training students from all parts of the world in a year's study at Addington Palace—perhaps leading to the Archbishop of Canterbury's Diploma in Church Music instituted in 1936; by refresher courses for organists and choirmasters, as well as for junior clergy and lay-readers; by summer schools for choristers and festivals of church music held in cathedrals, schools and other places. Furthermore, the new training scheme for choristers has enthused choirs with a renewed vitality and purpose. And many choirs in isolated parts of the world have benefited from the expert musical advice of one of the special commissioners.

Alongside the work of the R.S.C.M. exists the Church Music Society, which was founded in 1906. Its first president was Archbishop Lang who also became the first president of The School of English Church Music in 1927. The main aim of this Society is to facilitate the selection and the performance of church music most suited for Anglican worship, besides the publishing of music that is not available in more accessible form. In the past the Society has endeavoured to educate public opinion through its occasional papers on church music; but this is now done more effectively by the R.S.C.M.'s *English Church Music,* first published in 1963. The Society of the Friends of Cathedral Music was founded in 1956.

Twentieth Century Church Music

This century is experiencing a new reformation. Just as in the sphere of modern theology there has been a discarding of worn-out beliefs and the upholding of doctrines connected with the contemporary scene, so English church music has undergone a similar reformation. It has set about discarding second-rate music in favour of innovation in harmonic idiom and experimentation in new kinds of liturgical music. This same kind of change is also happening in the Roman Catholic Church, which is faced with writing new music for her vernacular services. And providing it supplies a definite need, the retention of the church music of the past is a good sign. As the author of the Epistle to the Hebrews so rightly remarks: 'The shaking of these created things means their removal, and then what is not shaken will remain. The kingdom we are given is unshakable; let us therefore give thanks to God, and so worship him as he would be worshipped, with reverence and awe' (12 : 27–8).

The utilization of ancient and modern idioms is very much evident in the church music of this century, which has seen a return to folk-song and the music of the Tudors, a discarding of the Victorian love for the strait-jacketed four-bar-unit, and the use of a tonality through the introduction of The Twelve-Note System as seen in Frederick Rimmer's anthem, *Sing we Merrily* (N, 1963) and Alan Ridout's *Evening Canticles of Twelve Notes* (SB, 1966). One might compare, too, the conservative *Versicles and Responses* of Dr. Bernard Rose (N, 1961) with the more *avant-garde* settings of Tony Hewitt-Jones (N, 1964) and Alan Ridout (SB, 1964), then one realizes that a musical revolution has happened within the sacred walls of our churches, which Dr. Erik Routley has called 'the shaking of the musical foundations.' In recent times much creative church music is being written by composers outside the confined space of the cathedral organ-loft, who have brought a breath of fresh air into our worship from the secular world of English music.

The Conservative Craftsman

CHARLES WOOD (1866–1926), the son of one of the lay-clerks at Armagh Cathedral, succeeded Stanford as the Professor of Music at Cambridge in 1924. He has a gift for writing austere music for the liturgy, e.g. Short Communion Service in the Phrygian Mode (FP, 1919), wherein the techniques of plainsong and contrapuntal music are combined. And he follows Stanford's method of writing an independent organ score for his *Collegium Regale Service* (AHC, 1932).

The anthem, *Glory and Honour and Laud* (AHC, 1925) forms a choral rondo. The trebles and altos respond to the other voices, sometimes dividing into three parts, e.g. 'Children before whose steps rais'd their Hosannas of praise.' Wood's harmonic gifts are best seen in the section, 'They to thee proffer'd praise for to herald thy dolorous Passion,' which ends with a fine *tessitura* at 'King on his throne.' The last section of this work is full of excitement, effected through the economical use of the voices which break forth from six-parts to eight-parts, but only coming together at the final cadence. A similar anthem is *'Tis the Day of Resurrection* (AHC, 1927), which divides into three movements and concludes with a brilliant modulation at 'Their notes let all things blend.'

O Thou the Central Orb (AHC, 1915) is distinctive for its movement in both the vocal parts and the organ score, which opens with a virile sound of octaves. The middle section has an effective bass entry, 'Come, quickly come,' and ends quietly with four notes sung in unison. There are many scintillating runs for the trebles, e.g. 'Hope soars above.' Another popular anthem is *Expectans expectavi* (AHC, 1919), in which there are twelve bars of organ introduction in order to set the devotional atmosphere of contemplation and intensity of human feeling. And the accompaniment is enhanced by eighteen bars of rest, so that in a moment of ecstasy the organ blazes out with the voices: 'To thy great service dedicate.' The text of this work is taken from a poem by a young man of very great promise, Charles Sorley, who died in action in France during the First World War.

Charles Wood is one of the pioneers of 'the hymn-tune type of anthem' that begins with the melody of a hymn-tune sung in unison. This is followed by a verse harmony, sometimes unaccompanied, and ends in unison with the organ weaving a descant above the voices. In this way Wood utilizes many of the old French and German tunes, e.g., *God omnipotent reigneth* (AHC, 1927), *How dazzling fair* (AHC, 1929), and *O Thou sweetest Source of gladness* (AHC, 1931).

RALPH VAUGHAN WILLIAMS (1872–1958), born at Down Ampney Rectory in Gloucestershire, was educated at the Royal College, where he studied under Parry and Stanford. At Cambridge he entered Trinity College and had tutorials with Charles Wood and organ lessons with Alan Gray. And in the summer months, he would travel to Ely to hear Choral Evensong on Sundays, although he was never a professing Christian.

He advocated congregational singing and the use of melody editions for hymn-singing. Yet his greatest gift to hymnody is the arrangements he made of the Genevan psalm-tunes and English folk-song melodies, thus extending the ancient custom of the church's use of secular music in the service of the sacred, e.g. the melody of *Forest Green* (EH 15) is derived from 'A Ploughboy's Dream' and that of *Monk's Gate* (EH 402) from the song, 'Our Captain Calls.'

Altogether, Vaughan Williams has written about fifty choral works—including *Five Mystical Songs* (SB, 1911), *Fantasia on Christmas Carols* (SB, 1912), *Sancta Civitas* (C, 1926), *Benedicite* (OUP, 1929), *Dona nobis Pacem* (OUP, 1936), *Prayer to the Father in Heaven* (OUP, 1948), *Hodie* (OUP, 1954), which contains the beautiful settings of 'The Blessed Son of God' and of his wife's poem 'No sad thought his soul affright,' and *A Vision of Aeroplanes* (OUP, 1956).

modern idiom of Benjamin Britten. Marked rhythms and cleanly-woven organ-accompaniments are found in his church music, as well as that sudden element of surprise in its climaxes, as if the doors of heaven were thrown wide in order to let the rays of the divine glory shine upon the faces of God's children.

Howells' choral music covers a wide field. The fine *Hymnus Paradisi* (N, 1950) was written in memory of his son and was first performed at the Three Choirs Festival. Its main theme is that of Light (*Et lux perpetua luceat eis*), which is very much evident in the dazzling *Sanctus* and in the final section wherein the souls of men are pictured as inheriting a home of unfading splendour. The *Missa Sabrinensis* (N, 1954) is unliturgical in length, comprising a hundred and ninety-nine pages of music, and contains far too many complex harmonies. A better work is the *Missa Aedis Christi* (N, 1961), where the composer has combined the flexibility of plainsong with the freedom of sixteenth-century polyphony. The *Stabat Mater* (N, 1964) was written for the Bach Choir in affectionate memory of Ralph Vaughan Williams, who shared with the composer his devotion to the composers of 'The Golden Age' of English music.

In November 1944 Howells began writing in Cambridge a collection of distinctive settings of the Anglican Canticles. In all of them people and places had a dual significance. His *Collegium Regale* was associated with Dr. Ord and Dean Milner-White and with King's College Chapel. Its setting of the *Evening Canticles* (N, 1950) was the original source of these compositions, having a feminine simplicity and scintillating treble passages that lift the worshipper's thoughts constantly upwards, as if the choirboys themselves were climbing heaven's ladder. A sense of urgency is evident at the beginning of his *Te Deum and Jubilate* (N, 1950), the setting of the latter work being noticeable for its un-inhibited joy—'O go your way into His gates with thanksgiving' and for its melismatic notes at 'World without end.'

To have written so many settings of these Canticles would have taxed many composers' ideas. Yet the *Worcester*

(N, 1963) is distinctive for its tender treatment and flexible vocal-writing; *St. Paul's* (N, 1954) for its broad texture and gradually-built climaxes — taking into consideration the accoustics of the building, as well as for the punctuating organ part in the Gloria very similar to Stanford's setting in C; *Westminster Abbey* (N, 1967) for its saraband rhythms and beautiful treble phrases; and *St. John's College* (N, 1958) for its quasi-plainsong writing and sensitive treatment of the Nunc Dimittis.

In 1941 Howells wrote *Four Anthems* (N, 1962), reflecting the troubled times of the Second World War and mankind's desire for peace. He displays a great sensitivity towards these texts from the Psalms and a romanticism in his enchanting melodies. His modernity in their musical texture is apparent in the climaxes, e.g. 'Thou art my King, O God' (*We have heard with our ears*), 'But it is thou' (from the same anthem), and 'Where is now thy God?' (*Like as the hart*). His fine *Coventry Antiphon* (N, 1962) rises nobly to the occasion of the consecration of the new Cathedral, as well as portraying the inherent power of the biblical text: 'An house of prayer *for all people,*' and 'The *glory* of this latter house shall be *greater* than of the former.' An abiding sense of religious atmosphere is seen in both the Motet, *Take him, Earth, for cherishing* (composed for the Washington Memorial Service to the late President Kennedy), and the *Three Carol Anthems* (SB, 1918): 'Here is the Little Door,' 'A Spotless Rose' and 'Sing Lullaby.'

SIR WILLIAM HARRIS (1883–) was a chorister at St. David's Cathedral in Wales. After a period as assistant-organist at Lichfield, he returned to Oxford to become organist at New College and later at Christ Church Cathedral (1928–33). He retired in 1961 from being the organist at St. George's Chapel, Windsor, after twenty-eight years' service. Harris is essentially a craftsman-composer in the tradition of both Stanford and Wood. Stanford himself might have written the motets, *Bring us, O Lord God* (N, 1959) and *Fair is the heaven* (AHC, 1925). And Charles Wood might have composed the hymn-tune anthem, *O what their joy* (OUP, 1931), with its unison sections and unaccompanied parts, such as 'Now in the meanwhile, with hearts raised on high.'

William Harris has composed some excellent hymn-tunes, e.g. *Alberta, Kybald Twychen, North Petherton, Petersfield, Sennen Cove* and *Stoner Hill,* as well as useful service music: *A Simple Communion Service* (RSCM), *Communion Service in C* (OUP) and the *Evening Service in A* (OUP). He wrote a lyrical setting for trebles of *The Lord is my Shepherd* (N, 1939) and two very fine extended anthems: *Ascribe unto the Lord* (N, 1948) for the 600th anniversary of the foundation of the Order of the Garter, and *Strengthen Ye the weak hands* (N, 1950) that was first sung in Canterbury Cathedral at the service commemorating the Science and Art of Healing in 1949.

The Modern and Experimental Composers

SIR ARTHUR BLISS (1891–   ), the Master of the Queen's Music since 1953, was educated at Cambridge, where he studied under Charles Wood. In his younger days Bliss was regarded as one of the most daring of our modern composers, having come under the influence of Stravinsky. But this earlier revolt against romanticism has somewhat declined; and his more recent music is decidedly romantic and pictorial, e.g. his Cantata *Mary of Magdala* (N, 1962), which has an atmosphere of expectancy in the orchestral accompaniment, portraying the running of the disciple's feet to the Empty Tomb; and *The Beatitudes* (N, 1962) that has many fine solo movements and opens with a scene of 'A troubled world.' For the centenary service of the Missions to Seamen, Bliss wrote a dramatic anthem with a powerful organ part, *Seek the Lord* (N, 1956), as well as another virile anthem for the reopening of Llandaff Cathedral *Stand up and bless the Lord* (N, 1960).

SIR WILLIAM WALTON (1902–   ) was educated at Christ Church, Oxford, where he had been a chorister at the choir school and had composed *A Litany* (OUP, 1937). Walton is a good example of a modern composer being invited to write special music for the church. Already in 1937 his *Belshazzar's Feast* (OUP) had caused a major stir in the musical world, when the conservative musicians were terrified by the music's sardonic flavour and full-blooded realism of the biblical narrative. This secular idiom invaded the Coronation Service of 1953 with the first performance of his *Te Deum* (OUP). But an even greater work was the *Gloria* (OUP, 1961), which was commissioned for the 125th anniversary of the Huddersfield Choral Society.

Most of Walton's choral music has been written for particular occasions, such as the Wedding Anthem *Set me a seal upon Thine heart* (OUP, 1938) and the *Missa Brevis* (OUP, 1966), which was commissioned by the Friends of Coventry Cathedral and is one of the best of the shorter Communion settings to have been published in recent times.

SIR MICHAEL TIPPETT (1905–), the Director of Music at Morley College until 1952, first came to the public's notice through his oratorio, *A Child of Our Time* (written in 1941; BH, 1944). It was an original idea to have included in this work five Negro Spirituals. The same year of this oratorio's first performance saw the first liturgical performance of his unaccompanied anthem, *Plebs Angelica* (BH, 1944), wherein the composer portrays the invocation of the angelic hosts with one section of the Canterbury Cathedral choir responding to the other.

His *Magnificat and Nunc Dimittis* (SCH, 1962) was commissioned by St. John's College, Cambridge. It is an electrifying work, with much use made of the *trompette real*. But this sounding-forth of the organ's Spanish trumpets is utterly out-of-keeping with the feminine mood of the biblical Canticle, even if this was intended to enhance the jubilation of the occasion—the 450th anniversary of the founding of the College! The Magnificat is marked by a lyrical style and particularly beautiful are the softly-sung treble and alto passages in contrast to the scintillating chromatic Gloria in 5/4 time. And Tippett's unusual treatment of the Nunc Dimittis is masterly. The organ accompaniment repeats a chord of four consecutive chromatic notes that is also imitated by the lower voices. And the virtuoso treble soloist weaves a melody over the rest of the vocal parts. The composer has clearly intended that the Nunc Dimittis should be contrasted to the jubilant Magnificat by emphasizing its note of renunciation. This modern setting is based upon The Twelve Note System.

BENJAMIN BRITTEN (1913–) was born on St. Cecilia's Day. He studied composition under Sir Frank Bridge and John Ireland. And his choral music forms a watershed in English music, being indebted to the past, especially to Purcell's *Sacred Songs* (1688 and 1693) which taught him the importance of brilliance, clarity and tenderness in musical composition. And it is also greatly influenced by the music of the moderns (e.g. Stravinsky) and the use of tonal effects:

> His work is full of experiments in sound which are wonderfully successful but leave one wondering whether they serve any end beyond themselves. Britten always appears to be intensely interested in the means by which music is produced, but not always so interested in the invention of significant material.[3]

An example of this experimentation is the Festival Cantata, *Rejoice in the Lamb* (BH, 1943), where the unusualness of the mad poet's vision is cleverly conveyed to the music, especially when the poet's Cat Jeoffrey worships God 'by wreathing his body seven times round with elegant quickness.' Thus the creative strength of Britten's music lies in his ability to transform traditional music into something that is new and abounding in vitality, which is superbly demonstrated in his treatment of the old carols in the Variations, *A Boy was Born* (OUP, 1934), that contains the beautiful *Corpus Christi Carol*.

[3] From *A General History of Music in England* by Ernest Walker (Clarendon Press, 1952), page 358.

I

A Ceremony of Carols (BH, 1942) was written for the choirboys of St. Matthew's Church, Northampton, and forms a sequence of medieval carols. It is characterized by sudden changes in rhythm and by its colourful harp accompaniment in the background. The opening theme and religious atmosphere are immediately set by the procession of choirboys chanting *Hodie Christus natus est.* Aud musical pictorialism is evident in the stillness of *In freezing Winter Night,* in the Lullaby *O my dear heart,* and in the final paean *Deo Gracias.*

The *Te Deum in C* (OUP, 1935) is an early work and is written in ternary form. Both the first and the last movements are based upon the chord of C major. The middle section is responsorial in form, but with all the singers coming together upon the word 'Judge.' However, a considerable advance in musical technique is seen in the *Festival Te Deum* (BH, 1945), composed ten years later. Britten employs in this work repeated chords in the organ accompaniment which later fan-out in massive ascending chords, introducing 'Thou sittest at the right hand.' There is variety in the unusual texture of 'Comforter' and in the rising chords of the Sanctus. Quick changes in the *tempo,* beautiful imitative melodies, a melismatic flourish at 'Glory everlasting,' and the inspired treble solo 'O Lord save thy people,' have made this *Te Deum* into an original work.

Britten delights in writing choral music for school children. The Cantata, *St. Nicholas* (BH, 1948) relates the story of this saint's birth, which is joyously greeted by a chorus of small boys singing in waltz-time and then interrupted by the tenor soloist's 'God be glorified.' Of particular interest are Britten's arrangements of well-known hymn-tunes and the dramatic realism of the billowy waves. Another Cantata, *Noye's Fludde* (BH, 1958) is based upon one of the Chester Miracle Plays. The composer's genius is evident in the use of handbells to portray a rainbow, as well as in the employment of the same notes for the Dove's return as for its outward journey; but this time played backwards! And there are arrangements of familiar hymn-tunes. He has also written a fine *New Year Carol* (BH, 1936) and a setting of *Psalm 150* (BH, 1950).

He has composed several anthems, including the eight-part *A Hymn to the Virgin* (BH, 1935), composed during his last year at school. Its simplicity and restraint are seen in the miniature-like phrases: *Tampia, Salutis, Rosa sine spina,* etc. Unity is achieved by means of an *ostinato* theme in the organ-pedal accompaniment throughout the *Hymn to St. Peter* (BH, 1955) and the *Hymn of St. Columba* (BH, 1963). Britten's finest anthem is undoubtedly the *Antiphon* (BH, 1956), written for the centenary of St. Michael's College, Tenbury. It is a majestic work in three movements. The introductory bars reiterate the word 'Praise'; and an antiphonal effect is created by the solo treble and the choir singing a group of contrasting phrases: 'Here below' and 'Here above,' 'To his friend' and 'To his foe,' etc. And it finishes with the usual Britten genius, with all the voices sounding together upon the word 'One'—whereas they had previously hovered upon 'One' and 'Two,' but each word sung separately by the two choirs. This same kind of imitative word-play occurs in *A Wedding Anthem* (BH, 1950), where 'These *two* are not two. . . . Love has made them *one.*'

The *Missa Brevis in D* (BH, 1959) is designed for a weekday celebration of the Roman Mass, when there would be only boys' voices available. This work is an example of a plainsong-like theme being sung in modern dress. New dimensions of sound are heard in the *Sanctus* and the *Benedictus qui venit,* when the *ostinato* semi-quavers in the organ part afford added brilliance to the Mass. And it was at the request of H.R.H. The Duke of Edinburgh that Britten wrote the *Jubilate Deo in C* (OUP, 1961) for St. George's Chapel choir. It is full of vitality, with bell-like semiquavers in the organ accompaniment. Tonal effects are created in the harmonization of 'For the Lord is gracious,' the quiet entry of the choir at 'Be ye thankful. . . . And His truth endureth,' and in the final battling of the Amens.

The famous *War Requiem* (BH, 1962) was written for the

Coventry Festival Celebrations of 1962. The text combined the *Missa pro Defunctis* with the anti-war poems of Wilfred Owen, who was killed in France. In this *Requiem*, tension is created by a full choir and orchestra set in contrast to the occasional sound of boys' voices accompanied by a chamber organ, portraying a scene far removed from the hubbub of the busy battle-front. The tolling of bells, the fanfares heralding the Day of Wrath, the leaping notes of the soprano's song of grief pleading for the divine mercy, the brilliance of the *Sanctus* supported by the percussion, the quietness of the *Benedictus* in contrast to the jubilant *Hosanna in excelsis*, all these differences have made this *Requiem* into the most profound choral work that Britten has written—enabling him to bring into prominence his great gifts for operatic writing, pictorialism in sound, and sensitivity to texts.

JOHN JOUBERT (1927), born in South Africa and now Lecturer in Music at Birmingham University, has written the austere anthem, *O Lorde, the maker of al thing* (N, 1953) and the fine Cycle of Motets, *Pro Pace* (N). The wide range of his musical activity can be seen in the tonal structure of the *Missa Beati Joannis* (N, 1962), the cheerful setting of *Welcome Yule* (N, 1957), the subtil word-painting of *Christ is Risen* (N, 1961) and the linear style of *The Holy Mountain* (N, 1964). The *Te Deum* (N, 1965) was commissioned for the centenary service of Malvern College; and his beautiful carol-settings include *A Little Child* (OUP), *There is no rose of such virtue* (N) and *Torches* (N).

KENNETH LEIGHTON (1929–) is now Lecturer in Composition at Oxford University. His church music belongs to the academic setting of the collegiate chapel with its highly-trained choir. An individualism is evident in his organ accompaniments, which weave intricate patterns of notes and have punctuating notes in their pedal-parts. Leighton has written two Cantatas: *Crucifixus Pro Nobis* (N) and *The Light Invisible* (N), besides an original setting of the *Coventry Carol* (N). His anthems are distinctive for their well-planned texture and abounding vitality, e.g. *Alleluia, Amen* (N, 1962), *Let all the world* (N, 1965), and *Give me the wings of faith* (N, 1962). The *Magnificat and Nunc Dimittis in D* (N, 1960) is an exciting setting with a virile chordal introduction on the organ that gives way to a lighter texture in the style of Howells. The Gloria of the *Nunc Dimittis* is characterized by its tranquillity. A more extended setting for concert performance is his *Missa Sancti Thomae* (N, 1966), which was commissioned by the Friends of Canterbury Cathedral to mark the 800th anniversary of St. Thomas Becket's consecration as Archbishop. It is distinctive for its changing moods, pungent harmonies, and for its closely-woven texture in both the vocal parts and the organ accompaniment.

There is every evidence that the future of Anglican church music is a bright one. Bernard Naylor has written some outstanding unaccompanied works, including the liturgical *Nine Motets* (N, 1960) and *Evening Canticles* (N). John Gardner has composed the *Cantiones Sacrae* (OUP, 1952), the *Mass in C* (OUP, 1966) and the *Jubilate Deo* (OUP, 1960). And Dr. Thalben-Ball has produced two useful collections of Introits, *Laudate Dominum* (N, 1954).

Moreover, the Australian Malcolm Williamson has written short cantatas in an original style, forming a bridge between the music of Britten and that of modern jazz. The merit of these cantatas—*Adoremus* (BH), *Harvest Thanksgiving* (W) and *Procession of Palms* (W)—is that they communicate a wonderful sense of joy to worshippers and have led more conservative composers to write in the same idiom, e.g. John Gardner's *Five Hymns in Popular Style* (OUP, 1963).

Conclusion

The history of English Church Music is the record of composers who have written liturgical music in the style of their times. And it was Archbishop Cranmer that insisted upon the intelligibility of the sacred text and the need for more congregational music. But the Anglican Church has been reticent in prescribing any definite rules concerning the use of music in worship, so much so, that it has refrained from authorizing any special hymn book for public use. The nearest one gets to an official view is the following statement from *The Report of the Committee appointed in 1948 by the Archbishops:*

> The music of the Church is therefore primarily the music that belongs to the Book of Common Prayer. The Prayer Book is based on the conception that it is the duty of the faithful to participate actively in the Common Prayer. The first duty of the church musician is to provide music that will aid this active participation.[4]

And these views are upheld by the Roman Catholic Commission for Liturgy's Report: *Instruction on Church Music* (1967), which states that the whole congregation should express its faith and devotion in song. But the Anglican *Report* would not go as far as to exclude polyphonic settings of the liturgy:

> The apostolic precept, to sing with the spirit and with the understanding, does not imply that all the music performed in church shall be of such a character that every member of the congregation should join in it vocally.[4]

At the same time, the Anglican *Report* qualifies this statement by maintaining:

> It is highly desirable that the music of those parts of the service which demand the vocal participation of the people should—especially in parish churches—call out congregational co-operation. The lack of the vocal response accounts for much of the listlessness that too often prevails in parochial worship.[4]

[4] From *Music in Church* (Revised Edition 1960: Church Information Office), pages 1–2.

But the Roman Catholic *Instruction* goes even further by maintaining that a sung liturgy is 'nobler' than a said one, because each group sings the kind of music that is proper to their activity; and what is more important, it affirms that the sung liturgy with full congregational participation effects a deeper union of hearts. This idea is ably elaborated by one of their liturgical scholars, Fr. J. D. Crichton, who writes:

> This is what the Christian faith is all about: *agape*, love, which is achieved and expressed by the drawing together of people into community. It is a human situation, for a congregation needs to discover the bonds of its unity in the process of celebration and there is no doubt that singing powerfully assists that discovery. It is certainly present in a said celebration, as we have known ever since the dialogue Mass began to be practised, but it was no itch for a better aesthetical expression of the celebration that drove people all over the Church to seek better ways and means of achieving and deepening the unity of the people at worship. This experience, too, was valuable since it indicated *the sort of music* that can do this. It was an essentially communal music not only in the sense that it enabled people to participate but also in the sense that it was apt of its nature to achieve this end.[5]

Fr. Crichton implores modern composers and choirmasters to take the trouble to understand that the real principles of liturgical celebration involve the understanding of the meaning and the nature of each sung part of the service. And it is the concern of the modern composer to express the feelings of adoration, contrition, forgiveness and thanksgiving in the music that he writes. It is fundamental that our worship should be a joyful and liberating experience, making our hearts overflow with that new song, 'Glory to God in the highest.' So Christians of every colour and race must sing:

[5] From *Liturgy* (The Quarterly of the Society of St. Gregory), No. 151, July 1967, page 59.

Let all the world in every corner sing,
　My God and King!
The Church with psalms must shout,
No door can keep them out;
But above all the heart
Must bear the longest part.
Let all the world in every corner sing,
　My God and King!

GEORGE HERBERT

For Further Reading

Apart from the books already mentioned in this Study, the following are also in print:

DAVIES, HORTON — *Worship and Theology in England* (Princeton, 1961–5): Vol. III, 'From Watts and Wesley to Maurice' (1690–1850); Vol. IV, 'From Newman to Martineau' (1850–1900); Vol. V, 'The Ecumenical Century' (1900–65).

DEARNLEY, CHRISTOPHER — *The Treasury of English Church Music Vol. III: 1650–1760* (Blandford Press, 1965).

HUTCHINGS, ARTHUR — *Church Music in the Nineteenth Century* (Herbert Jenkins, 1967).

JACOBS, ARTHUR (editor) — *Choral Music* (Penguin Books, 1963).

KNIGHT, GERALD and REED, WILLIAM (editors) — *The Treasury of English Church Music Vol. IV: 1760–1900; Vol. V: 1900–1965* (Blandford Press, 1965).

LE HURAY, PETER — *Music and the Reformation in England, 1549–1660* (Herbert Jenkins, 1967); *The Treasury of English Church Music Vol. II: 1545–1650* (Blandford Press, 1965).

LEWER, DAVID — *A Spiritual Song: The Story of the Temple Choir* (The Templars' Union, 1961).

MACDERMOTT, K. H. — *The Old Church Gallery Minstrels* (S.P.C.K., 1948).

ROBERTSON, ALEC — *Music of the Catholic Church* (Burns & Oates, 1961).

ROUTLEY, ERIK — *The Church and Music* (Duckworth, 1967); *The English Carol* (Herbert Jenkins, 1958); *The Music of Christian Hymnody* (Independent Press, 1957); *Twentieth Century Church Music* (Herbert Jenkins, 1964).

SCHOLES, PERCY A. — *The Oxford Companion to Music* (OUP, 1963); *The Puritans and Music* (Russell & Russell, 1962).

STEVENS, DENIS — *The Treasury of English Church Music Vol. I: 1100–1545* (Blandford Press, 1965).; *Tudor Church Music* (Faber & Faber, 1966).

Consult also *The Pelican History of Music* (Penguin Books) and *The New Oxford History of Music* (OUP).

Within the small compass of this book, it has been impossible to outline the history of the English Carol. The modern liturgical use of carols began at the end of the last century at Truro, where a service of nine lessons and carols was devised by the Vicar Choral. This liturgical pattern was modified by the late Dean Milner-White, who was also responsible for the familiar Bidding Prayer first read in King's College Chapel on Christmas Eve 1919. For further information, readers should consult the numerous writings of Dr. Erik Routley, Richard Greene's *The Early English Carols* (Clarendon Press, 1935), Reginald Nettel's *Christmas and its Carols* (Faith Press, 1960), and Douglas Brice's *The Folk Carol of England* (Herbert Jenkins, 1967).

Index

142

Date Due

AP 11 '83			
MAY 1 2 1988			
		.	

Demco 38-297